**Sandeep Nulkar** is a veteran of the translation industry in India and one of its more known faces globally. The first Asian to receive the 'Outstanding Contribution to the Language Industry' award, Sandeep has also been named among the Top 50 global localisation influencers by Nimdzi. He serves on the National Executive Committee of the National Language Translation Mission set up by the Ministry of Electronics & IT, Government of India, and leads initiatives as the co-chair of two committees at FICCI. Sandeep also contributes on several advisory boards and is presently the vice president of the Alliance Française, Pune. He is a popular columnist and author who is currently working on his first fiction novel and has been commissioned to write two film scripts.

# MIND IT!

**A TONGUE-IN-CHEEK LOOK AT HOW
INDIAN ENGLISH CAN AMUSE AND EVEN CONFUSE**

## SANDEEP NULKAR

RUPA

Published by
Rupa Publications India Pvt. Ltd 2024
7/16, Ansari Road, Daryaganj
New Delhi 110002

*Sales centres:*
Bengaluru Chennai
Hyderabad Jaipur Kathmandu
Kolkata Mumbai Prayagraj

Copyright © Sandeep Nulkar 2024

The views and opinions expressed in this book are the
author's own and the facts are as reported by him which
have been verified to the extent possible, and the publishers
are not in any way liable for the same.

All rights reserved.
No part of this publication may be reproduced, transmitted,
or stored in a retrieval system, in any form or by any means,
electronic, mechanical, photocopying, recording or otherwise,
without the prior permission of the publisher.

P-ISBN: 978-93-6156-297-6
E-ISBN: 978-93-6156-465-9

First impression 2024

10 9 8 7 6 5 4 3 2 1

The moral right of the author has been asserted.

Printed in India

This book is sold subject to the condition that it shall not,
by way of trade or otherwise, be lent, resold, hired out, or otherwise
circulated, without the publisher's prior consent, in any form of
binding or cover other than that in which it is published.

*To every English-speaking
Indian with a sense of humour*

# Contents

*Preface*   *xi*

1. A Slap in the Face — 1
2. A Girl Named Call — 3
3. Again and Again — 5
4. Brother from Another Mother — 7
5. Busy Bees — 12
6. And Let There Be Light — 15
7. A Grand Welcome — 16
8. Back to Square One — 18
9. Be a Darling! — 21
10. Brilliant Students — 24
11. Catching Something, Are We? — 27
12. Chew and Chomp — 29
13. Being Too Aware — 31
14. Days Too Many — 33
15. Class Act — 35
16. Commercial Concerns — 37
17. Cool, Soft and Hard Stuff — 41
18. Cut! Cut! Cut! — 43
19. Discussions Galore — 45
20. Eating Out — 48
21. Did Someone Just Faint? — 50
22. Dead Serious — 52
23. Dial 'M' for Murder — 54
24. Die Hard — 56
25. Do What? — 58

| | | |
|---|---|---|
| 26. | *English Vinglish* | 60 |
| 27. | Give Me a Break(up) | 62 |
| 28. | Divorced or Still Together? | 64 |
| 29. | Eat All You Can Drink | 66 |
| 30. | From Side to Side | 68 |
| 31. | Going Out(side) | 70 |
| 32. | Fill It Up! | 73 |
| 33. | Giving or Taking? | 76 |
| 34. | I, Me, Myself | 79 |
| 35. | Full Stops, Abbreviations and More | 81 |
| 36. | Googled, Xeroxed and More | 84 |
| 37. | High Maintenance | 86 |
| 38. | Hilarious? Not Quite! | 88 |
| 39. | Gone Too Soon | 90 |
| 40. | I Will Go. I Will Come Back. | 93 |
| 41. | Job Hunting | 95 |
| 42. | Keep It Back | 97 |
| 43. | Last Man Standing | 99 |
| 44. | Lucky Me | 101 |
| 45. | Lunch in a Box | 103 |
| 46. | Insistence Unlimited | 105 |
| 47. | Kindly Please | 108 |
| 48. | Meet and Greet | 111 |
| 49. | Nothing to Worry About | 113 |
| 50. | Meatily Amusing | 115 |
| 51. | Movie Magic | 117 |
| 52. | Ms Julie | 119 |
| 53. | Let It Be! | 121 |
| 54. | Like How? | 123 |
| 55. | Mobile Mania | 125 |
| 56. | Of(f) and Away | 127 |
| 57. | On and Off | 129 |

| | | |
|---|---|---|
| 58. | Out of Thin Air | 131 |
| 59. | Parts of Indian Cars | 133 |
| 60. | Means to an End | 136 |
| 61. | Mornings, Afternoons and Evenings | 138 |
| 62. | Past Perfect | 140 |
| 63. | On Our Own Trip | 142 |
| 64. | Passing the Parcel | 143 |
| 65. | Petrol Problems | 145 |
| 66. | Picture This | 147 |
| 67. | Tickets and Us | 149 |
| 68. | No Lights | 152 |
| 69. | Ruled by the Ruler | 155 |
| 70. | Perfecting Our Pronunciations | 157 |
| 71. | Pressure Cooker | 159 |
| 72. | Pretty Cars | 161 |
| 73. | Shifting Out | 163 |
| 74. | Please Don't Kill Anyone | 165 |
| 75. | Rest in Peace | 167 |
| 76. | Sit and Do What? | 170 |
| 77. | Sex | 173 |
| 78. | Repeat Offenders | 175 |
| 79. | 'Sixteen Going on Seventeen' | 177 |
| 80. | So Fresh | 179 |
| 81. | Such a Comprehensive Bath | 181 |
| 82. | Small Small, Different Different | 183 |
| 83. | Staying Abroad | 185 |
| 84. | Tring! Tring! | 188 |
| 85. | Sunny Side Up | 191 |
| 86. | The Action Continues | 193 |
| 87. | Sweet Tooth | 196 |
| 88. | Take It or Leave It | 198 |
| 89. | Take Your Pick | 200 |

| 90. | We Are Like That Only | 202 |
|---|---|---|
| 91. | Very Costly Indeed | 205 |
| 92. | What Sound Was That? | 207 |
| 93. | Testing Times | 210 |
| 94. | The Both-Handed Writer | 212 |
| 95. | Thank You | 213 |
| 96. | The Art of Gifting | 215 |
| 97. | The Great Indian Bobble and Other Gestures | 217 |
| 98. | What's in a Name? | 219 |
| 99. | When Will We Reach? | 221 |
| 100. | Who Came and Where? | 223 |
| 101. | The Silent Admirer | 225 |
| 102. | The Number Game | 227 |
| 103. | The Opposite Need Not Always Be True | 229 |
| 104. | Whistle *Podu* | 231 |
| 105. | Word to Word and Same to Same | 232 |
| 106. | Whose Son Is He Anyway? | 234 |
| 107. | Ya-Ya Land | 236 |
| 108. | *Yeh Dil Mange More* | 238 |
| 109. | Toilet Woes | 240 |
| 110. | Yes and No | 242 |

| *Acknowledgements* | 245 |
|---|---|
| *Glossary of Grammatical Terms* | 247 |

# Preface

If a film like *Hindi Medium* managed to strike a chord with the audience even in this day and age, you can imagine the aspirational value that English must have enjoyed all along. From being used as a language that facilitated working with and pleasing our British 'masters' once upon a time, to becoming a qualification that lands us better jobs and helps us climb the social ladder today, English has ruled the collective conscience of a country that can itself boast of numerous indigenous languages and thousands of prevalent dialects.

Even when I was growing up, things were not very different. It was a commonly held belief in society that those who studied in vernacular-medium schools could probably not speak English even to save their lives, whereas the more 'fortunate' ones who went to English-medium or convent schools spoke great English. Belonging to the 'fortunate' category, I was raised on a staple of praise for my impeccable English. Living in that bubble was so comforting, I tell you.

But, finally and thankfully, my bubble burst at the turn of the century when I first visited London. My English, that was supposed to be impeccable, suddenly seemed very different for the most part and even inadequate every now and then. And then, something else happened on this trip that made me look at English very differently.

While browsing through dictionaries at the famous Grant & Cutler bookshop in Central London, the name of a certain dictionary caught my attention. It was an 'English to American' dictionary. Such was their linguistic pride that the

British seemed unwilling to acknowledge American English as English. For them, it was simply 'American'. By that logic, I thought, what we speak would be called 'Indian' and that it might not be all that 'English'.

My initial (over)confidence was quickly replaced by a deep desire to observe how we Indians spoke and how that was different from how the natives spoke. Languages being my profession, it was hardly surprising that I found my observations useful. What was surprising, however, was how people around me did not find my observations boring. In fact, they quite enjoyed listening to the many peculiarities of Indian English that I used to talk about, and peculiarities there are many.

Over the past two decades, I have come across thousands of peculiarities in the way we speak English, and they all have great entertainment value. But that is not the only reason why we should know about them. We live in an increasingly global world, where work and travel require us to rub shoulders with people from different nationalities. Globally, people are generally more accustomed to native English than they are to the Indian dialect. And that is fine. It does not mean that there is something terribly wrong with our dialect.

In fact, I am immensely proud of how Indian English has contributed to the English language or even sadistically happy about how it has sought colonial revenge. However, the problem with dialects, ours included, is that using them outside their locale can get us into potentially embarrassing situations, like the one I nearly got into once, sitting comfortably in my office in Pune.

It had only been a week since Trushna had joined our company when she needed to use the fax machine. It was not something we needed often. So it was kept in a corner and could only be accessed from behind my chair. Since Trushna was still getting to know all of us, she probably felt a little awkward asking me to get up so that she could pass. Instead, she simply squeezed herself through the tiny gap between the back of my chair and the wall.

Squeezing herself through that gap must have clearly been way more uncomfortable than asking me to get up was awkward because, once she was done using the machine, she mustered the courage to ask me to let her pass. However, what she said to me in Marathi was 'Sir, सोडा ना (*soadaa na*) please!' If someone who spoke my dialect of Marathi would have heard her say that without having us in their field of vision, they would have probably thought that I had grabbed her in an inappropriate way, and she was pleading with me to let her go. In her dialect, however, that was a perfectly normal way of asking someone to make way.

The point is, using dialects outside their locale is ill-advised. The only option we have then is to speak 'neutral' English, a version of English that is devoid of Indianisms and thereby closest to what the world in general will understand. The dictionary defines Indianisms as words or idioms that are characteristic of Indian English. However, for the purpose of this book, I would define Indianisms as words and idioms that reek of poor grammar, terrible usage, or both, and are something we must endeavour to rid our English of.

This book is a collection of some of the most classic Indianisms—the ones that are influenced as much by our mother tongues and our abject ignorance of grammar as they are by our innate ability to coin words when we do not know or cannot think of the right one. They have been curated from among the thousands of Indianisms that I have come across over the past two decades.

This book is meant to inform and entertain, not to create the pressure to learn or remember. So, enjoy it much before you use it to change the way you speak. After all, there is nothing wrong in speaking Indian in India, because *we are like that only, no?*

# 1

## A Slap in the Face

Trust me when I say that I have complete authority over this slap business. I have been at the receiving end of so many from my parents and teachers that, at some point, I had even started believing that it was a necessary step in raising children. I mean, how much can you beat up a poor child, granted that I wasn't exactly the neighbour's envy or even the owner's pride? But all this beating was for nothing, it seems. It wasn't even the right kind of slap.

You see, I was always asked if I wanted 'one tight slap'. It was a trick question, as I was to realise later. No matter how I answered the question, I received one anyway. Nonetheless, the entire process was made to look very democratic, even though it always resulted in the reddening of at least one cheek. And then to my deep chagrin, as education cleared the clouds of ignorance, I realised that a 'tight slap' doesn't even exist!

I don't know why Indians love to call it a 'tight slap'. There is nothing actually tight about it. And yet, there was an entire movement built around it, where a tight slap was offered to every person who said politically incorrect things on social media. Native speakers of English and most of the Western world will have no clue what sort of a slap a tight one might be because they have 'hard slaps', not tight ones. They use 'hard' as an adverb that qualifies the verb 'slap'. For example:

*'The officer slapped him hard.'*

So, how did we Indians manage to convert the slap from a 'hard' one to a 'tight' one? Me thinks the answer lies in the act itself. When Indian parents and teachers ask the rhetorical question about whether the child wants a slap, the hand is always held firm, in a right angle, with fingers joined together tightly. Perhaps that is why it came to be called a 'tight slap'. However, when native speakers call it a 'hard slap', they are referring to how hard you are going to be hit. Trust me, I know! It always felt hard, not tight.

Speaking of slaps, did you know that the phrase 'a slap in the face' has got nothing to do with an actual slap? It simply means 'an unexpected rejection'. And surprisingly, 'to slap someone on the back' is neither a slap nor a rejection. It actually means 'to congratulate someone'. I certainly wish I had got more of those when I was in school.

## 2

## A Girl Named Call

Indian brains work in mysterious ways. I have travelled to over a dozen countries and seen hundreds of people add mobile numbers of new contacts to their phonebooks. But nowhere in the world have I seen a method for adding contacts quite like the one we have invented. And if need is indeed the mother of all invention, then we Indians seem to have taken this need to heart and the invention to a whole new level.

I am talking about mobile phones and the amazing concept of giving someone a 'miss' call. As innovative as the idea is, it can be very amusing for a native speaker of English for a couple of reasons. Firstly, to most minds that aren't aware of what it means, and heard without any context, a 'miss call' sounds more like 'Ms Call' (a girl whose surname is Call). Secondly, it is droll how we think we can actually 'give' it to someone.

Technically, a 'missed call' is a recipient's thing, not something we can 'do' (or 'give') on purpose. We can only end the call before the recipient answers it. That would still only mean that we 'called' (or 'ended the call'). It is the recipient who would have missed our call. So, you can only 'see' missed calls on your phone, not 'give' or 'receive' them.

Most importantly, it is grammatically incorrect to say 'miss call'. In English, there are many ways to form adjectives[*] out

---

[*] To know the meaning of the grammatical terms, turn to the Glossary at the end of the book.

of verbs. One of those ways is by adding the suffix '-ed' to a verb. So, the verb 'miss' becomes an adjective only after we add the suffix '-ed' to it. Therefore, the adjective is 'missed' and not 'miss'. So, what people refer to as a 'miss call' should actually be a 'missed call'.

Here is some trivia about missed calls to end this story about Ms Call with. Although missed calls are especially prominent in India, they are widely used in most emerging markets, where people opt for prepaid plans that allow only a limited number of minutes for outgoing calls. From being used rampantly in marketing and even in social activism to becoming an easy way to communicate a pre-decided message, missed calls are perhaps one of the smartest ideas of our times.

# 3

# Again and Again

I know this will sound a little far-fetched, but let's pretend it's actually happening. Imagine you are watching an artist's concert somewhere in London. Let's say it's Adele, singing her heart out, belting out one brilliant number after another. At some point, you are so touched by her rendition of the number 'Hello' that you let out two loud cheers: 'Once more! Once more!'

Those seem to be some kind of magic words because, at that very moment, everyone in the hall turns to look at you. People seem bemused and Adele seems to be even more perplexed, unable to comprehend what exactly she is supposed to do next. And you seem to be the most baffled soul in the hall, unable to fathom why everyone reacted in that way.

So, let's analyse what just happened here. When you shouted 'once more', people found it to be extremely out of place. Well, not the fact that you shouted, but what you actually said, and ergo all the attention you got in this story of ours.

Native speakers of English simply do not use 'once more' in the sense of the audience calling for a repeated or additional performance of a number at the end of a concert. The phrase means something completely different to them than what it means to us. When native speakers are bowled over by someone's performance and want to request them to perform once again, they simply say 'encore'.

But this is also where we need to be extremely practical about things. Neither Adele nor a concert in London might be a part of our reality, but we could find ourselves at a concert in India, and we certainly don't want the entire hall staring at us, trying to figure out what we meant by our prudish chant of 'encore'.

If you look up the meaning, you will notice that 'once more' is a phrase that is used when we want to suggest that something was done or happened 'one more time' or 'once again'. It is used in situations such as when a teacher says to her student:

*'You aren't getting it. Let's try this once more (or one more time).'*

Or perhaps when someone says:

*'I would like you to explain this to me once more.'*

'Encore', on the other hand, is a French word that means 'again'. It is used to request an artist to repeat a part of their performance. It is used as a noun, an exclamation and a verb. For example:

*'The artists got up on stage for an encore.'*

Or,

*'The audience shouted, "Amazing! Encore!"'*

Or,

*'Nearly all the songs that Lata sang were encored by the audience.'*

I am sure you have heard what they say about doing what the Romans do when in Rome. That applies to India too. When in India, go with what works here, but when you step out of the country you now know exactly what you need to say.

# 4

## Brother from Another Mother

India breeds and how! At over 30 babies per minute[*], every single day, without a single day of rest, we have bred over a billion people. That is a lot of people, a staggering number of relationships and an awful lot of work.

I mean, if we have so many people, we will obviously have an equally high number of relations. And then, we also need to name those relations, because Indians don't exactly believe in living very private lives. The smallest of occasions, and we can easily get a few dozen relatives to assemble in one room. Such frequent social interactions are probably why we felt the need to have personalised names for every relation. It is not surprising then that most Indian languages will have different names for the different types of brothers, sisters, uncles, aunts and even grandparents.

So, while our mother's sister's son is our 'मौसेरा भाई (*mausera bhai*; literally, brother by virtue of being the son of our mother's sister, or *mausi*)', our father's brother's son is our 'चचेरा भाई (*chachera bhai*; literally, brother by virtue of being the son of our father's brother, or *chacha*)' in Hindi. English, however, dumbs all this down to the word 'cousin'.

The word 'cousin' itself means a child of one's uncle or

---

[*] '"30 Children Born per Minute in India": Union Minister Giriraj Singh Calls for Population Control Bill for All Religion', *Firstpost.*, 27 November 2022, https://tinyurl.com/f37sejvh. Accessed on 13 May 2024.

aunt. Again, English does not distinguish between our father's brother and mother's sister, or our father's sister and mother's brother. All are simplified as 'uncle' or 'aunt', whereas in most Indian languages, these relations have different names. And this is practically how it goes for the tons of relations we have. In our mother tongues, every relation usually has a unique name, depending on their paternal or maternal lineage.

Little wonder, then, that we Indians feel extremely inadequate when forced to simply call someone our 'brother', for example. That also probably explains why we feel the need to prefix some adjective to the noun 'brother'. After all, how do you satisfy the urge to explain to someone that a certain person is not just another brother, but a brother born of the same parents? And hence, even though this practice might be alien to the English language, you will find many Indians say:

*'He is my real brother.'*
[Read: We are brothers born of the same parents.]

Doesn't this remind you of the 'सगा भाई (*sagaa* bhai; literally, brother born of the same parents)' as they say in Hindi or the 'सख्खा भाऊ (*sakkhaa bhau*)' as they say in Marathi, or something similar in most Indian languages? Well, that is the mother-tongue influence playing out in plain sight.

Then, we also have a similar problem with the word 'cousin'. In most Indian languages, the parallel word for 'cousin' will either be masculine or feminine. In English, however, be it a boy or a girl, they are both just 'cousins'. The lack of clarity about the gender is probably what makes us want to suffix the words 'brother' or 'sister' as adjectives to the noun 'cousin'. It is, therefore, very common to hear Indians say 'cousin brother' or 'cousin sister'. But there are no cousin brothers or cousin sisters in English.

For whatever they are worth, all these are still genuine relations. But it's amazing how quick we are to forge relations with just about anyone. So, from the auto-rickshaw driver who drops our children off to school and random friends of our parents, to our neighbours and anyone who we ever cross paths with, in India, everyone who is much older than us is either an uncle or an auntie, or a brother or a sister if they are much younger. And if we can't place them adequately, we often go with the more impersonal 'sir' or 'madam', as we can't exactly call them by their first names.

In the West, however, the system is very different. Uncles and aunts, much like brothers, sisters and cousins, are people you are actually related to. You don't call them that just to give them respect or to make them feel like a part of your family. Most importantly, the word 'aunt' precedes the name of the aunt. So, unlike in Indian English, where we might have a 'Sangeeta auntie', native speakers of English have an 'Aunt Gertrude' and not 'Gertrude auntie'. Incidentally, 'auntie' is not a very commonly used word outside India, apart from the fact that it is also very informal.

As for 'sir' and 'madam', we really need to be careful with their usage. In English-speaking countries and especially in the United Kingdom (UK), 'sir' and 'madam' are indeed used as a polite or respectful way of addressing someone. For example:

*'How may I help you, sir?'*
Or,
*'How may I help you, madam?'*
[Note that the 's' or 'm' are not capitalised.]

'Sir' is also used to address someone in a position of authority, apart from being a title that is used before the forename of a knight or a baronet. For example:

> *'Sir Isaac Newton is widely recognised as one of the most influential scientists of all time.'*

'Madam' is also used before a title to refer to a female holder of a certain position. For example:

> *'I now request Madam President to address the audience.'*

But mind it, used in isolation, one of the possible meanings for the word 'madam' could also have a different connotation. It could mean a woman who runs a brothel, or it could also be used informally to mean a woman who is conceited or bossy.

Speaking of 'madam' and 'sir', I cannot help but think of any other Indianism that wins the race of amusing others, and that too by a distance. As if things weren't already complicated enough, we even added a hint of patriarchy to the mix inadvertently. I am talking about a certain web series on Netflix, where Shefali Shah's character is referred to by her juniors not as 'madam' but...hold your breath for this one... 'madam sir'! And we cannot even put this down to creative liberty taken for the reel life; people say it in real life too.

And while we are at it, let us also single out 'boss' and 'ji' as two more words that we need to stop using pronto, especially when speaking to non-Indians. Yes, I know, our culture does not allow us to call people by their first names and that we need to use some word to show our love, respect and affection for people. But when speaking English and especially when referring to foreigners, the use of 'ji', as in 'Trump ji', ends up sounding more funny than respectful.

As for 'boss', that's a different story altogether. In India, we use the word 'boss' casually, when we want to get someone's attention, or even as a replacement of the millennial 'bro'. But, for heaven's sake, please don't go around calling random people 'boss' when travelling to other countries. From finding it odd to downright condescending, depending on the cultural sensibilities of a place, you never know how people will take it.

Understanding relations and according respect accordingly might be complex in India, but is not quite so as far as English is concerned. So, when speaking English, remember to keep it simple!

---

### 'Anyways'

'Anyways' is an American's idea of slang and an Indian's idea of acceptable English. Sadly, there is no such word in 'real' English. The 's' is unnecessary because adverbs do not have plurals in English. The right word is 'anyway'.

# 5
## Busy Bees

When I was learning French back in the late 1980s, our teacher used to be this wildly funny person. The students adored him because his class was nothing short of an entertaining stand-up act.

One day, when he was teaching us the past tense, he asked the students to narrate what they had done the previous evening. Knowing that an incorrect answer would most certainly result in some theatrics, a girl tentatively mumbled in French how she had watched a certain show '*sur la télévision* (literally, on the television)'.

This incorrect use of a preposition worked like the perfect cue for our animated teacher to launch into a dramatised performance. He promptly climbed on the chair and looked 'on' top of the gigantic television that lay on the table and announced to an amused class:

*'I can't seem to find any programme "on" this television!'*

Be it French or English, using all the right prepositions in all the wrong places is totally our thing. So, when a friend once told me that he would not be able to meet up with me because he was expecting some guests and that he was going to be busy 'in that', I could not help but smile to myself thinking how this teacher of ours would have enacted such a prepositional misadventure.

In English, one can never be busy 'in' anything. What

could have given rise to such usage is probably a similar sentence construction in many Indian languages. Here are some examples:

उसमें व्यस्त रहूँगा *(usmay vyast rahoongaa;* literally, Hindi for 'will be busy in that')

તેમાં વ્યસ્ત રહીશ *(temaa vyast rahish;* literally, Gujarati for 'will be busy in that')

However, saying 'busy in that' is wrong. One can be busy 'in the day' or even 'in one's field of work'. However, one cannot be busy 'in that'. That makes no sense. 'Busy' is usually used directly with the present participle, for example:

*'I am busy planning my daughter's wedding.'*

You can also use 'busy' with the prepositions 'at' and 'for'; for example:

*'I have been so busy at work lately that I hardly get any time to exercise.'*

Or,

*'Don't waste my time. I am too busy for all this.'*

You can also use the preposition 'with' with 'busy'; for example:

*'What are you busy with these days?'*

Or,

*'We have really been busy with the twins.'*

And while we are on the topic, let me warn you to be a little careful when using the verb–noun collocation 'get busy'. Although people might not misunderstand you, unless there is that kind of a context to what is being spoken, the informal meaning of 'to get busy' is to have sexual intercourse. The formal meaning of 'to get busy', however, is to begin working on something that needs to be done.

Take a deep breath, give it some thought or consult a dictionary if you must, but make sure you get these right. Because you can never be too busy to use the right prepositions!

# 6

## And Let There Be Light

Globalisation was thrust upon a country that was only just waking up to modern life. Our economy opening up was not magically going to produce all the electricity we needed to play with the fancy gadgets we now had access to. I grew up in an India where power cuts were as common as the common cold. Since power cuts were not restricted to daytime alone, one always needed something to light up the nights.

Depending on the family's affluence (or the lack of it), every household had candles, oil lamps, lanterns or torches. Again, depending on one's linguistic affluence or the lack thereof, a 'torch' was also referred to by many as a 'flashlight' or a 'battery'. To most Indians, these might seem like interchangeable nouns even today. Unfortunately, that's not the case.

A 'torch' ('flashlight' in American English) is a portable electric lamp that is powered by batteries. Some people even refer to 'batteries' as 'cells'. Technically, this is not the right thing to do. These are not interchangeable nouns. A 'cell' is a unit in a device that converts chemical energy into electrical energy. A 'battery' is a collection of one or more cells. A cell alone might not be able to power devices but a battery can.

So, the next time you walk into your local 'electrical' (and not 'electric') shop, try asking for some batteries (that you now know run on cells) to power your torch.

# 7

## A Grand Welcome

I get how we Indians take a lot of pride in being extremely welcoming people. However, some people tend to take this tag a tad too seriously. I mean, being warm and all is fine, but leaving proof of it all around the house is almost like giving our guests constant reminders of how hospitable we are. Have you ever noticed the sheer number of items that some houses have that stand testimony to this trait?

There is that trademark doormat with the word 'welcome' occupying nearly its entire length and breadth. Then, as if the size of those letters is not enough to drive home the message, you will also find the classic wall-hanging—the one with a lady, with palms folded to form Namaste. And thereafter, the creative field opens up. From *toran*s (decorative door hangings) and door signs to keychain stands and curios, the golden word can be found on many an object.

And just when you think you have seen it all, you realise you have also seen the word spelt differently, often with some grammatical bloopers. 'Wel-come', 'well-come' or even 'well come' are just the few examples I can think of, off the top of my head. You might have seen some others too. And then, there is also the confusion about the right conjugation when more than one person is welcoming us, for example, to a wedding.

The fact is that 'welcome' can be used in many ways.

As a noun:

*'He received a warm welcome.'*

As a verb:

*'Mr and Mrs Sharma welcome you to the wedding.'*

Or as an adjective:

*'This was a welcome change.'*

In no case, however, can 'welcome' be spelt any differently than the whole of it together. As for the conjugation bit, the verb will always be spelt as 'welcome', barring in the third-person singular ('he', 'she' or 'it'), where it will be spelt as 'welcomes'.

Now, go check how 'welcome' has been spelt on your doormat and any other curios that might sport it.

# 8

## Back to Square One

It looks like corporate India takes human beings to be some kind of objects. Surprised? Me, not quite! If one uses words meant for objects when referring to human beings, then such a conclusion is only a hilariously logical corollary.

Pick any one of the millions of linguistically challenged emails flying across the corporate world, and chances are that you will find something in it that has sentences like these:

*'Please revert back at the earliest.'*
*'If interested, please revert with your updated CV.'*

And this is precisely where the problem lies. The verb 'revert' simply means to return to a previous state, practice, topic, etc. In that sense, what these sentences would actually mean to a native speaker of English is:

*'Please return back to your previous state at the earliest.'*
*'If interested, please return to your previous state with your updated CV.'*

Now, would you not agree that a native speaker of English might find this to be somewhat funny, and perhaps even a little confusing? These sentences can simply be constructed in this manner:

*'Please reply at the earliest.'*
*'If interested, please send us your updated CV.'*

Unless you intend to poke fun at someone by saying how the person raised one leg and then lowered it back to its original position—whereby the leg can be said to have 'reverted' to its original position—'revert' is a verb that is best used in the context of objects or things, and not human beings. Here are a few examples to help you understand where and how this verb can be used:

> 'The watch <u>reverts</u> to normal operation if no key is pressed for three seconds.'
>
> 'After the vending machine has dispensed a bottle of water, it <u>reverts</u> to the standby mode.'
>
> 'Although he did speak very good English, he found the need to <u>revert</u> to his native language every now and then.'
>
> 'Although mass religious conversions were reported, it was also said that some people <u>reverted</u> to their former religion.'
>
> 'The deal did not go through and the ownership of the property was <u>reverted</u> to its former owner.'

Even in the above examples, remember to never use the adverb 'back' after the verb 'revert' because it already has the sense of 'to return to' or 'to go back to'. 'Revert back' would be a sort of a pleonasm.

When it comes to language, less can also be more. Beauty can lie in minimalism too.

### 'Avail'

'To avail' means to use or to take advantage of, but only to Indians. To the rest of the world, it means to help or to benefit. And saying 'avail an offer', like we do in India, is wrong because one cannot help or benefit an offer. One avails oneself of something, for example, 'We availed ourselves of the offer.'

# 9

# Be a Darling!

This happened in the summer of 1991. Philippe, a French student, was visiting Pune as part of the Indo-French student exchange programme and was staying with me and my family. Although his days were packed with tons of activities, we always made it a point to eat dinner together.

Dinner-table conversations were fun. Philippe always had very interesting observations about India and Indians, and it was amusing to learn how foreigners viewed us. Speaking of amusing, I still remember this one conversation that had left all of us in splits. As usual, Philippe was telling us about what he did that day, when he said that he thought Indians were extremely open-minded people. When we asked him why he thought so, he explained, 'I see so many gay men on the street, walking with their arms around each other's shoulders and some even openly holding each other's hands. This is very surprising for me because in France we are just about beginning to warm up to the idea of men having such preferences and we don't see too many same-sex couples display this kind of affection openly on the street.'

His words acted like a trigger. Almost everyone at the table burst out laughing. I then explained to Philippe how it wasn't uncommon to find teenagers and sometimes even grown men doing this in India. I told him that it was their way of bonding, of telling each other that they were indeed very close friends, and it was not always a sign that they were gay.

But, come to think of it, these can indeed appear as strange habits to someone whose culture is very different. Men putting their arms around each other's shoulders, holding hands and sometimes even landing hurried pecks on the other's cheek aren't uncommon sights in India, as much as they would mean different things to Westerners.

Indian men seem to go particularly wild with such gestures when they feel an uncontrolled or sudden burst of 'bromance'. Such feelings typically surface in places more commonly known as relaxing tourist spots, like Goa, or when men are high on alcohol or life, or even when they are being jerks and passing lewd comments on other people's mothers and sisters.

Indianisms need not always be verbal. Foreigners can find it difficult to interpret some of our actions too. And as if our actions aren't confusing enough, we add to the imbroglio with our verbal creativity.

Take the obsession of many Indian men to overuse the word 'dear', for example. Let's accept it. The Brits know when and how to use it, and especially when elderly British women use the word, it sounds extremely warm—endearing even. However, when Indian men end sentences with 'dear', it comes across as, at best, corny and at worst, cheesy. It's probably our accents or simply because we use the word incorrectly.

In general, we should avoid using the word 'dear', especially when travelling outside India. It might come across as condescending, bizarre, or both. The right place and reason to use 'dear' is at the end of a sentence and as an affectionate or friendly form of address when speaking to someone not older than them. For example:

*'I will take care of this. Don't you worry, dear.'*

But do you know who actually steals the show? Hands down, it's those Indian men who take this creativity and confusion to a whole new level by calling their male friends 'darling'. I have a few friends from up north, who call me 'Sandy darling'. I know it's only out of love, but not all foreigners would know how to interpret that.

# 10

# Brilliant Students

I have seen three types of parents. There are some who make the word 'understated' look understated. They will simply never be found praising their children. They are, of course, one extreme of the spectrum.

On the other end, there are those who leave no opportunity to chirp and twitter (yes, that is a verb too) about their children. No matter what you say about your children, these parents have this extraordinary ability to connect it back to their children, and how, in fact, theirs are better at the thing being discussed.

Most others fall somewhere in between. They aren't as unfair to their children as the understated variety, nor are they as toxic as the 'twitterrati' who make you want to run away.

I am regularly invited by schools, universities or other organisations to speak about my profession. That has also given me the opportunity to interact with hundreds of students and their parents across the country. I have thereby been privy to the one mistake that seems to be common throughout, irrespective of the type of parent I am speaking to. It is how they speak about the grades their brilliant children have got.

> 'Sir, he has got <u>out of</u> marks in French.'
> 'Sir, she has always been a <u>rank holder</u> in all her courses.'
> 'Sir, my son has scored <u>cent per cent</u> marks.'
> 'Sir, my daughter <u>came first</u> in her class.'

These are some of the ones I get very frequently. I am sure you, too, would have heard some or all of these. However, none of these are correct, for a variety of reasons.

First and foremost, the fictional adjective 'out of' exists only in Indian English. It would mean nothing to anyone who is not used to how we speak. Getting 100 marks out of 100 does not mean you got 'out of' marks. It simply means you got 'full marks' on an exam.

Then, if you say someone is a 'rank holder', native speakers of English would invariably think of an army officer and surely not of a student. If you top the class, it does not mean that you are a rank holder by virtue of getting the most marks. It just means that you have always been among the top three in your class. As for 'coming first' in a class, let us not even get started with such linguistic atrocities.

Lastly, a little about 'cent per cent'. It actually is just about the usage. Native speakers will simply never say that someone got 'cent per cent marks', even though 'cent per cent' does mean 100 per cent. That is perhaps because 'cent per cent' also has the sense of 'complete' or 'total' and you would never say someone got 'complete marks'.

And just so you know, 'marks' and 'grades' are not interchangeable nouns. A 'grade' is more like a category that is expressed as A, B, C, etc. 'Marks', on the contrary, are scores that are expressed in numbers. Marks in a certain range might mean a certain grade. For example, marks between 90 and 100 might mean an A+ grade. Sometimes, schools prefer grades over marks so as to take the pressure off students.

So, do your brilliant children some justice by announcing their achievements using all the right words.

### 'Backbenchers'

In India, 'backbenchers' would be those dudes and dudettes in school or college who grew taller but not necessarily smarter. In British English, it is not even a word used for an average person. It actually means a member of the British Parliament who does not hold office in the government or opposition and who sits behind the front benches in the House of Commons.

# 11
## Catching Something, Are We?

You puff and pant as you run alongside the majestic Mumbai local. You squeeze yourself through the mere millimetres of space left by the descending passengers. You push through, still puffing and panting. You finally make your way to what looks like an empty seat. But alas! A smarter ass, taking aim from the train window, has managed to land his handkerchief on what could've been your seat.

I have heard of dogs marking their territory with urine, but humans and handkerchiefs! Not surprising actually. Desperate times do call for desperate measures. In a land of too many people and not enough seats, 'catching' a place is indeed a national contest.

But come to think of it, there are only so many things we can 'catch' in life. As babies, we catch a cold as easily as we catch butterflies when we grow slightly older. Then, as teenagers, a few lucky ones get to catch a movie with that special someone, much like how those busy climbing the corporate ladder might catch their breath after climbing a few steps, with little time to spare for any physical activity.

Be that as it may, the fact is that humans are not capable of 'catching' a place, not in English at least. But that does not stop hundreds and thousands of Indians from asking their friends and family to 'catch' a place for them. The reason it seems right to us in Indian English is probably because of the way it is said in most Indian languages. Here are some examples:

जगह रोकना (*jagah rokna*; literally, Hindi for 'to stop place')
जागा पकडणे (*jaagaa pakadnay*; literally, Marathi for 'to catch place')

So, when we want to say this in grammatically correct English, it suddenly becomes a Herculean task for most Indians. The uninitiated will go with the usual:

*'Will you catch a place for me, please?'*

The slightly more initiated might try to impress with the more dignified:

*'Will you reserve or book a place for me, please?'*

Beyond that, people will simply hit a roadblock. Thankfully, we don't yet get to hear a Hindi-inspired:

*'Will you stop a place for me, please?'*

But then, how does one say 'jagah rokna' or 'jaagaa pakadnay' in English? The answer is pretty straightforward actually. You simply use the verb 'save' and form the question. Here are a few examples:

*'Could you save me a seat, please?'*
*'Could you save us some seats, please?'*

But don't you try this on unsuspecting Indians. They might not get you. This usage is strictly reserved for your trysts with foreigners, or when you want to show people how good your own English is, or when you are speaking to someone with impeccable English. In India, keep it simple. Speak Indian!

## 12

# Chew and Chomp

What do I say about the travails of a stay-at-home mother? There is already so much to do in the kitchen, and then, there are the in-laws, the husband and, of course, the perpetually hungry children to take care of.

So, you can imagine the plight of the mother when these hungry little scavengers start rummaging for food in every container they can lay their eyes on, only to find nothing. Continue to scavenge and rummage they do, but now, the target is their mother. A few minutes of incessant demands later, the mother usually loses her mental and emotional balance and howls:

*'Stop eating my head, please!'*

As much as we can empathise with the poor mother, on a linguistic level this is at best cute and at worst totally wrong. 'To eat someone's head' is inspired by how this is said in most Indian languages. Here are some examples:

दिमाग़ खाना (*dimaag khaana*; literally, Hindi for 'to eat brain')

तकली खावाप (*takli khaavap*; literally, Konkani for 'eat head')

But then, the million-dollar question is how do you say this in correct English? Well, one can simply say:

*'Stop pestering me!'*

Or,

*'Stop nagging me!'*

But mind it, the phrase 'to pick someone's brain(s)' has a very different meaning. Do not confuse it to mean 'to pester' or 'to nag'. 'To pick someone's brain(s)' means to obtain information by questioning someone who is better informed about a subject than oneself.

---

### 'Pester Power'

You know how some kids can pressure their parents into buying things that they have seen in advertisements on television or elsewhere? Well, there is actually a term for that. It is called 'pester power'. Ever wondered why there are so many children in advertisements today? Well, now you know!

## 13

# Being Too Aware

I have had an extremely turbulent relationship with dog signs. Anyone who is genuinely petrified of dogs would. I have entered houses despite being warned by those wretched signs, only to find myself being eyed hungrily by a delighted alpha dog. The look in those canine eyes always betrayed the owner's assurances that theirs was the sweetest dog in town and meant no harm.

There are dog signs such as:

*'Never mind the dogs. Beware of the owner!'*

Or,

*'I can make it to the fence in 2.6 seconds. Can you?'*

Or,

*'Is there life after death? Jump the fence and find out.'*

I have seen some funnily scary dog signs while travelling across England. Back home, however, dog signs are a different deal altogether. Whether or not they are creative or funny, they surely are matter-of-fact and scary. And, of course, they make for great grammatical hunting grounds too.

Apart from the usual 'beware of dog' warning, I have seen numerous permutations and combinations of this hostile message. 'Be ware of dog', 'Be-ware of dogs' and even the rare 'Be aware of dog' are some that have accompanied the image of a fierce-looking hound. But the jury is certainly not out on this one.

The grammatically correct thing to say is 'beware of the dog', although some native speakers can be found giving the 'the' a miss for reasons of brevity or space. If you have two dogs, the right thing to say would be 'beware of the dogs'. The definite article 'the' is needed because we are warning people about a specific dog, and not just any dog.

And oh, pretty please, let us be aware that 'be aware' and 'beware' do not mean the same thing. While the latter is a verb that means to guard against or be cautious and alert to dangers, the former is an adjective that means being conscious of or having knowledge of a situation or fact. When it comes to grammar, a little space can make a big difference!

# 14

## Days Too Many

How Mrs Bindra loved to brag! And that's the thing with braggers, right? Nothing is ever too trivial to be used as a brag topic, especially when you have a high-net-worth bloke for a husband. So, whether it was that expensive trip they took or that important business trip her husband's company sent him on, everything had major brag value.

What stayed with me more than the topics our former neighbour bragged about, however, was how she always talked about that fabulous '10-days' package to some place or that important '2-days' business trip her husband 'had to' take to Paris. I hope you are getting the drift because that is not how you say it in English.

The instinct of anyone who has ever studied even the most rudimentary form of English grammar would be to use the noun 'day' in its plural form. Logically and grammatically, if there are more than one, then they have to be referred to as 'days' and not 'day', right? But as always, looks are indeed deceptive and things are never as they seem in English.

So, here's the thing. In English, when you use a 'number–noun + noun' kind of a construction, the number–noun combination actually becomes a hyphenated compound adjective, which is an adjective that comprises two or more words separated by a hyphen. And since adjectives do not have plural forms in English, there is no question of adding an 's'.

By the way, hyphenated compound adjectives need not always involve a number. That is why you can sit at your 4-ft table, write a convincing 2-page leave application letter, go on that once-in-a-lifetime 10-day holiday to Krabi and laze around on the sun-kissed beach.

# 15

## Class Act

Be it for the skewed student–teacher ratio, for the desperation to give our children that competitive edge, or for the scant confidence we have in the ability of our institutions to deliver quality education, the flourishing coaching-classes industry in India points to a systemic rot of epic proportions.

In a country where Kota is unfortunately as famous for its coaching classes as Agra is fortunately for the Taj Mahal, there is hardly a student who has not succumbed to the coaching-classes mania. Hoardings attempting to portray these classes as a magical key to success, clutter the landscape of nearly every city.

But the term 'coaching classes' exists only in Indian English. The word 'coaching' itself means the act of giving special classes, which makes the word 'classes' following it redundant. And calling them 'classes' is wrong too. The word 'classes', used by itself, simply does not have the meaning that we have attributed to it.

A class is a group of students who are taught together. A class can also mean a lesson, which is a period of learning or teaching. That is why you can say things like:

*'I am late for my music class.'*

Or,

*'I take classes in classical music.'*

Or,

*'I give classes in English.'*

However, you cannot run an institute with a name like 'Sandeep's Classes' or 'Sandeep's Coaching Classes'.

What we refer to as 'classes' is simply a 'private tuition'. It is called 'private' because the teaching that happens when children are in school or in college is actually 'mass' tuition.

And mind it, teachers giving private tuitions are not called 'tuition teachers'. That, too, happens only in Indian English. Native speakers call them 'private tutors'. And private tutors will teach no more than a few students at a time, not hundreds of them as is prevalent in our 'coaching classes'.

I hope all private tutors in India read this and rush to the nearest shop to get a new signboard designed for their institute. More than anyone else, we need them to first get their terminology right!

# 16

# Commercial Concerns

Indian offices are like war zones when it comes to English. And since everything is indeed fair in love and war, the belligerent Indian professional wields his linguistic sword, showing no mercy to those at the receiving end of their verbal onslaught. Words are cobbled together, much like politicians cobble up a majority. It makes no difference whether the words even exist in the English language or whether what is being said would even be understood globally.

Let us take three unique situations to understand how this verbal onslaught pans out. The first one is when the Indian professional seeks to understand the cost of a certain product or service. For instance, look at this sentence that is used in practically every office across India:

*'Once your sample has been approved, we will discuss the commercials.'*

To begin with, there is no such word as 'commercials'. The closest word you will find is 'commercial', which is an adjective that surely does not have the intended meaning. When people in our country say 'commercials' they mean discussing, negotiating and agreeing on the price of sale. 'Commercial' does not have that meaning.

The more creative ones also use the word 'financials' instead of 'commercials'. Fortunately, the word 'financials' exists. Unfortunately, it does not have the intended meaning either.

It simply means the finances or financial situation of an organisation or individual, or the shares we hold in financial companies. It is, therefore, best to say:

> *'Once your sample has been approved, we will talk about the prices.'*

The second situation is when an Indian professional tells you how to send them such a commercial proposal. That is when you will get to hear a sentence like:

> *'You can email your best offer to Ramesh at the rate of thebestcompanyever dot com.'*

The problem with the sentence is how people enunciate the '@' symbol. The '@' symbol is actually a logogram for the word 'at' and not for 'at the rate of'. Yes, this symbol does have the sense of 'at the rate of', especially when you are expressing a cost per unit, for example in a sentence like this:

> *'I bought 7 kg of apples @ ₹100 per kg.'*

However, using 'at the rate of' when telling someone your email address is funny because you are not really expressing a cost per unit here. The '@' symbol in an email address has a very technical meaning. It means that the recipient (in this case, Ramesh) is not the local host, but is at a different host (in this case, thebestcompanyever.com). So, the right way to say this would be:

> *'You can email your best offer to Ramesh at thebestcompanyever dot com.'*

As for the last situation, it is when the Indian professional incurs out-of-pocket expenses. That is when you will probably hear a boss tell his subordinate something like:

> *'Please pay for these expenses by cash. I will make sure Accounts refunds them to you at actuals.'*

This sentence is a virtual goldmine of Indianisms. To begin with, one does not pay 'by cash'. It probably seems right because one can pay 'by cheque'. However, as far as cash is concerned, one always pays 'in cash' (not even 'pays cash').

Then, saying 'Accounts' is fine as long as it is in an informal conversation. If it is a formal or a written communication, it might be prudent to say 'the accounts department'.

As regards the word 'refund', it is not the same as 'reimburse'. You can refund the money if a customer is not satisfied with the goods or services they purchased. But, if you are simply repaying a person for the expenses they incurred on your behalf, then you are 'reimbursing', not 'refunding'.

As for 'at actuals', it is a very Indian thing to say. Neither will you find it in any dictionary, nor will you find any native English speaker using it. When we say 'paid at actuals', what we mean is that the cost, whatever it may be, will be reimbursed. Here is how this sentence should actually be phrased:

> *'Please pay for these expenses in cash. I will make sure that the accounts department reimburses the actual cost of your expenses.'*

Modern workplaces are truly cosmopolitan. Even if your workplace does not have people from different nationalities, chances are that you will still find yourself interacting with professionals from all across the globe. The corporate Indian needs to get their English right, now more than ever before. Let's say, this chapter could be the beginning.

### 'Batchmate'

A word that is used in India to refer to someone who was never your classmate but was in a different section of your class during the same academic year. A word that might not be understood internationally, unless people can extrapolate the logic from classmate. You can simply say that you were in the same year as someone.

## 17

## Cool, Soft and Hard Stuff

My earliest memory of a cold drink is of this vendor walking through our train compartment, carrying a crate loaded with glass bottles that contained some colourful drinks. Those chilled bottles looked so heavenly, and the sound of his bottle opener clacking against the bottles so musical. The next thing my poor mother knew, she was being pestered by me until a bottle was thrust in my hands.

Kids are particularly crazy about cold drinks. The lure of cold drinks can get children to study, behave or do whatever their parents fancy. Given the copious amount of sugar cold drinks contain, and how that lights up the reward centres of our brains, it is hardly surprising that the craze continues even today. What is surprising, however, is how our favourite cold drink is always a Coke, a Pepsi or some other carbonated drink. Why is it never lime juice or Rooh Afza with lots of ice?

Well, that could be because in Indian English we refer to 'soft drinks' as 'cold drinks'. But technically, any drink that is 'cold' is a 'cold drink'. A 'soft drink', on the other hand, is a non-alcoholic drink containing carbonated water, a sweetener and some artificial flavouring. And strangely, although we do not quite use the word 'soft drink' (which exists), we have no qualms using the word 'hard drink' (which does not exist).

The word 'hard drink' is purely an Indian invention, by the way. It is possibly based on the logic that if a drink with no alcohol is a soft drink, then a drink with alcohol must be a hard drink. But it does not work like that. The globally-accepted word for 'hard drinks' is 'spirits' (a strong distilled alcoholic drink) or 'hard liquor' (anything above 20 per cent alcohol by volume).

What is also an Indian invention is the word 'peg'. Native English speakers simply order a drink, and the standard serving size in most countries that I have visited is 50 ml. There is no concept of a 'large peg' or a 'small peg' like there is in India. So, ordering large or small pegs when travelling abroad will only get you blank looks, not alcohol. However, a 'single' or a 'double' are legitimate options in most countries.

There is something else you should never ask people when travelling abroad. Asking for directions to the nearest 'beer bar' or 'permit room' will also be met with blank looks. These exist only in India and in Indian English. Westerners simply have 'bars' that are more about the alcohol and less about the food.

Now, if this looks like too much information to process, go fix yourselves a drink, raise a toast, say cheers and make merry! It will all come together after a good night's sleep.

# 18

## Cut! Cut! Cut!

The English we speak is so deeply influenced by our mother tongues that I think we subconsciously end up choosing words or collocations that reflect this influence. It is almost as if our brains go from thinking of something to say in our mother tongue to translating that into English, before ending up blurting out a sentence that is at times nothing more than a literal translation.

That is perhaps what happened to this certain mother who was whining about how her son would have actually scored way higher than what he actually did, had his teacher not 'cut his marks' for his shabby handwriting.

Where do you think we picked up this usage from? Peek into the way you would say it in your mother tongue and you would perhaps find the culprit. Here are some examples:

> Marks काटना (marks *kaatnaa*; literally, Hindi for 'to cut marks')
>
> Marks কাটতে (marks *kawtawtay*; literally, Bengali for 'to cut marks')

It is no wonder then that we feel there's nothing wrong in using the verb–noun collocation 'to cut marks'. But then, if this is not how it is said, how does one say it correctly in English? Well, in English no one can 'cut your marks', you actually end up 'losing marks'.

This mother would have therefore been better off saying:

*'My son lost marks for his shabby handwriting.'*

But what if she actually wanted to blame the teacher? Clearly, saying 'cut his marks' was out of the question. How else could she have said it then? Native speakers of English put it really well when they say:

*'The teacher marked him down for his shabby handwriting.'*

There, you now know all the possible options. And yes, one last thing before we put a lid on this topic for good. Although in India students 'get good marks', in the English-speaking world children 'score well'. Different but easy, right?

# 19

# Discussions Galore

We all know how confused we Indians can be when it comes to the use of prepositions while writing or speaking English. For most Indians, 'on' and 'above' are interchangeable, and that may also be the case with 'below' and 'under'.

It is no wonder that we end up using the wrong preposition every now and then; we use none when one is needed or use one when none is needed. The preposition that we are going to learn more about in this chapter falls under this last category—using one when none is actually needed.

Quite a few would raise their hands if I were to ask whether many of you have heard or said something like:

*'We will meet and discuss about this in person.'*

A large number of us would either not find anything fundamentally wrong with this sentence or even actually be convinced that this is how it is said.

The reality, however, is different. The verb 'discuss' does not need the preposition 'about'. In fact, it does not need a preposition at all. 'Discuss' is a transitive verb. Transitive verbs are action verbs with a direct object. They do not need any prepositions. For example:

*'Ronaldinho kicked* (transitive verb) *the ball* (direct object).'

There is no need for a preposition here and hence we do not say:

*'Ronaldinho kicked to the ball.'*

The urge to use 'about' after 'discuss' probably comes from the fact that 'about' is used after similar action verbs such as 'talk', 'debate' or 'have a conversation'. However, these are intransitive verbs.

The urge also perhaps comes from how we say this in our mother tongues. Here are some examples:

के बारे में चर्चा करना *(ke bare mein charchaa karnaa;* literally, Hindi for 'to talk about something')

च्या बद्दल बोलणे *(chyaa baddal bolnay;* literally, Marathi for 'to talk about')

But the correct way to say this is:

*'We will meet and then discuss this in person.'*

That being said, one can use the preposition 'about' after 'discuss', but that is only if it is used in the noun form 'discussion'. These examples will help you understand this better:

*'We had a discussion about politics.'*
*'We discussed politics.'*

I am going to leave you with a seemingly confusing (against the backdrop of what we discussed above) yet fun sentence I came across in *The New York Times*, dated 24 November 2006:

*'On average, Keller Fay finds that people <u>discuss about</u> a dozen brands each day.'*

Although here it does seem like the preposition 'about' has been used after the verb 'discuss', in reality, that is only because in this case 'about' has not been used as a preposition but as an adverb that means 'approximately'. You will understand the construction of this sentence and get its meaning if you read it this way:

*'On average, Keller Fay finds that people discuss approximately a dozen brands each day.'*

## 20
## Eating Out

Not so long ago, I chanced upon the catchy Bollywood number that goes '*kisi disco mein jayein, kisi hotel mein khayein* (literally, Hindi for "let's go to the disco, let's eat at a hotel")', from the film *Bade Miyan Chote Miyan*. While I must admit that my two left feet did start moving to the beats, I could not help but wonder how the ravishing Raveena and the gyrating Govinda were actually guiltier of an Indianism than of public display of affection, or PDA. I am no purist really, but if we are talking about how Indian English can confuse, then this one can surely qualify as one of the better examples. I am talking about how people tend to use the words 'hotel' and 'restaurant' interchangeably. We have all been asked where a certain hotel is located or been told how the food at a particular hotel is to die for. Furthermore, the names of some restaurants actually start with the word 'hotel'.

The truth is that a hotel and a restaurant are very different things. While a hotel primarily provides accommodation, a restaurant offers food and drinks. I used the word 'primarily' because it is also possible for a hotel to provide food and drinks, provided there is a restaurant inside the hotel.

Then, some people also goof up when it comes to using the right prepositions to go with these nouns. The uncomplicated truth is that while we stay 'in' a hotel, we always eat 'at' a restaurant.

And while we are at it, let us also understand what a 'motel' is. Well, a motel is a roadside hotel designed primarily for motorists, having rooms arranged in low blocks with the parking directly outside the rooms. And then, there is also the 'inn', which is a pub in up-country areas that might sometimes even provide accommodation.

But who are we kidding? All this information aside, the song in question would probably not have sounded that great had the lyricist used the word 'restaurant' instead of 'hotel'. If you enjoy the song, grammar can always take a temporary backseat!

---

### 'Can I?'

A question that starts thus will almost always be replied with a 'yes, you can, but you may not' in every school worth its salt. 'Can' shows possibility, whereas 'may' seeks permission. You 'can' do something because it is physically possible for you to, but you 'may' not because someone forbade you to do so.

## 21

# Did Someone Just Faint?

Looks like getting an education and becoming unconscious make for strange bedfellows as far as Indians are concerned. The number of Indian students who unfailingly experience this scary state seems to be alarmingly high. It is perhaps time we addressed this once and for all. Wondering which of the many Indianisms am I talking about? Read on to get to the bottom of this mystery.

The bone of contention seems to be with the whole 'I passed out' thing that we tend to say after we are done with our last year in a school, college or university. When asked what one is currently doing, a very common and even acceptable answer in India could be as follows:

*'Nothing as yet. I just passed out of college.'*

The problem is that there is no guarantee this will be understood very easily beyond our borders.

'To pass out' primarily means to become unconscious. The sense in which we use 'pass out' would, however, be conveyed best if we were to use the verb 'to graduate'. You would therefore be better off saying that you 'graduated' from college, as opposed to saying you 'passed out' of it.

But as it is English, cometh the rule, cometh the exception. That is perhaps why the British do use 'to pass out' in the sense we do, but mind it, only in the context of the armed forces or the police force. For example:

*'Anand passed out of the NDA in 2024.'*

No surprises there. After all, the forces do have their own way of doing things, whether in life or language.

## 22

## Dead Serious

Some Indianisms have become such an integral part of mainstream discourse that we do not even suspect that the usage might be incorrect. Take for instance the word 'serious'. We do use it right in most cases. However, there are times when logic suddenly deserts us, and we use it to describe someone's medical condition.

I am sure we have all heard people talk about how someone in their family is 'serious' and has therefore been admitted to a hospital. However, if you tell that to a native English speaker, their first reaction would most probably be asking what the person was serious about and not the expected 'Oh God! I am sorry to hear that'.

You see, a person can surely be 'serious' ('dead serious', if you will). However, that will still not, in any way, mean that the person is ill (or even dead). It would only mean that the person is not joking or that the person is acting or speaking sincerely and in earnest.

When Indians say that someone is 'serious', what we actually mean to say is that the condition of that person is serious. So, why do people simply not say that then? It might perhaps have come from saying someone is 'seriously ill', which is grammatically correct, and over time, people simply switched to saying 'serious' instead of 'seriously ill'. I also have a feeling it has got to do with how we speak.

We Indians have this habit of throwing in one or two

English words when speaking in our mother tongues. And perhaps we find it easier to use a single English word (serious) than using a few (condition is serious) in the middle of a sentence that is otherwise being spoken in our mother tongues. However, it is important that we remember that it is not the person who is serious but their condition that is serious, or in some situations even critical.

Come to think of it, 'critical' is an equally apt or perhaps even a better word to use in such situations. It means that something has the potential to become disastrous. After all, when we say 'serious', don't we mean that the condition can escalate to be disastrous or life-threatening?

To be understood clearly in most places outside India and by most non-Indians globally, the right way to say this would be:

*'His condition is very serious.'*

Or,

*'He was brought to the hospital in a critical condition.'*

Indian English is perhaps a different language in itself and one that I am immensely proud of. However, how we speak should depend on who we are speaking to. That means, as right as our English might be for us, sometimes we simply need to know how to say things the way native English speakers do.

## 23

# Dial 'M' for Murder

Most parents would sell their souls to see their babies sleep peacefully at night. For sleep-deprived parents, already on the edge owing to weeks of insomnia, sleep rituals surrounding babies are a touchy topic. From the routine lullabies and hammocks to the more traditional nutmeg and milk, ideas come by the dozen in India. But it can never hurt to compare notes with other parents, can it?

So, when my wife's American friend was visiting us many years ago, we asked her what they did with their daughter Rita, who was nearly the same age as our daughter. To our utter surprise, she said they simply close the door to their daughter's room and let Rita self-soothe.

Self-soothe?! That is too barbaric for us to even imagine, right? Indian parents would never be able to leave their children to cry through the night. As shocking as that might seem to us, there is something we often say that can come across as equally shocking to a native speaker of English.

Every night, somewhere in India, a parent sings a lullaby or rocks a hammock in the hope that it will help their child fall asleep. But ask them what they are doing, and they are likely to say:

*'Oh, I am just <u>putting my baby to sleep</u>.'*

'Goodness gracious! Putting your baby to sleep? You can't be serious!' a Brit might retort.

The clueless Indian parent would be left wondering as to what part of the sentence the Brit might have found to be so shocking. But that is only because we lend our own meaning to words and phrases without really caring about their actual meaning.

Pretty much any dictionary will tell you that the phrase 'to put someone to sleep' means to make someone unconscious by using drugs, alcohol or an anaesthetic, obviously not something any Indian parent intends to do to their child. And yet, we say it.

Perhaps that is what foreigners mean when they say there is a method to the madness when it comes to Indian English. We begin by wanting to say something but end up saying something that has a completely different meaning. Yet, we are understood perfectly well by fellow Indians.

However, native speakers do not 'put their babies to sleep'. They simply 'put them to bed'. And, as a matter of fact, if you 'put an animal to sleep', it actually means you killed an old, sick or badly-injured animal in a painless manner.

Talking about killings, I cannot help but think of this unique Indian concept of bumping off alleged criminals without a fair judicial trial. We call it an 'encounter' or an 'encounter killing' in Indian English. However, in native English, there neither exists a word for such cruelty, nor would a native speaker understand us if we were to use such a term.

So, be mindful of what you say to a native English speaker. You might just end up saying something that is understood very differently or, worse still, not understood at all.

# 24

## Die Hard

From existing as animate beings to becoming completely inanimate objects—yes, some Indianisms have the power to bring about even that kind of a transition!

Now, how on earth is that even possible, you might wonder. Well, the recipe is fairly simple, you see. We take a harmless, regular verb such as 'expire' and (mis)use it in a sentence. And lo and behold, we have managed to do the impossible.

Going by the rules of English grammar, usually products expire. We can therefore have contracts that will expire, we can have medicines that would be well past their date of expiry, or someone's term of office might expire too. However, using the verb 'expire' when it comes to human beings is grammatically inhuman. We humans 'die'. At best, we 'pass away', but we do not exactly 'expire'.

That being said, the verb 'expire' was indeed used in the context of human death, but that was centuries ago. It finds its origin in the Old French verb *expirer* that means 'to expire' or 'to elapse' (used in the twelfth century), and in the Latin verbs *expirare* or *exspirare* that mean 'to breathe out', 'to blow out', 'to exhale' or 'to breathe one's last'. That is the reason it came to be used figuratively in the sense of 'to die'.

The verb 'expire' has the sense of to go beyond the due date or to come to an end gradually. But since humans do not exactly have a known due date and since we do not gradually come to an end, it is best we refrain from using this verb in the context of human deaths.

I know old habits die hard, but it always helps to keep it simple! If you ever need to break the terrible news of someone's death, you could just go with the regular 'he/she passed away last evening', or simply stick to 'he/she died last evening'.

And by the way, the phrase 'die hard' has got nothing to do with dying. It actually means to disappear or to change very slowly, like in the case of the phrase 'old habits die hard'.

Now, you might want to go check your passport, your licence, your subscriptions, and what have you. It is better to have them renewed, just in case they are going to expire anytime soon.

## 25

# Do What?

Why one thing, Indians can do two things too. In fact, we can even do three or four things. We are very efficient people, you see. But God knows why, ever so often in India, we are asked to only 'do one thing'.

Sample this! Somewhere in India, amid all the hustle and bustle, you are looking for this place that you don't seem to find despite activating all your intuitive geolocation powers. Tired of fighting this battle all by yourself, you finally decide to seek help and ask a passer-by for directions. Pat comes the helpful reply that goes something like this:

> '*Do one thing. Go straight, turn left and then...*'

I am sure there are numerous other occasions when we have heard or even used this classic Indianism—'do one thing'—although it seems like we use it mostly when we are making plans or offering advice to someone who is making the plans.

And since we love both, making plans as well as offering advice, sentences like these make their way to our everyday conversations:

> '*Do one thing. You pick up Rahul and reach the venue by 8.00 p.m.*'
> '*Let's do one thing. Let's not invite Nisha at all.*'

However, native speakers of English do not use such a phrase. So, where did we pick this up from then? Well, 'do one thing' probably stems from our habit of starting sentences with a similar phrase in most Indian languages. Here are some examples:

तू एक काम कर *(tu ek kaam kar;* literally, Hindi for 'do one thing')

ಒಂದು ಕೆಲಸ ಮಾಡಿ *(ondu kelsaa maadu;* literally, Kannada for 'do one thing')

Obviously, such a phrase isn't quite needed in English and needless to say, it will, in all probability, not even be understood internationally.

So, what do you say if you are feeling a little fidgety or verbally incomplete, for not having started the sentence thus? Well, you could try something as simple as:

*'Here's what you could do. Go straight, turn left and then...'*

However, when I think of what all the good Samaritans who helped me find addresses in London on numerous occasions said to me, I remember them commencing the sentence directly, without using such 'starter' phrases. So, that is an option too.

And yes, please don't be unreasonably allergic to this Indianism, because although 'do one thing' is wrong, 'do <u>this</u> one thing' is perfectly legitimate. You will find it in practically every listicle that starts with headings such as:

*'Do this one thing to lose weight.'*

Or,

*'Do these five things to be successful.'*

Enough of 'doing one thing' then. Let's just do the right thing and say things the way they were intended.

# 26
## English Vinglish

The very popular movie *English Vinglish* only highlighted what many Indians consider to be a fairly legitimate way of speaking. I mean, it would have sufficed to call the movie 'English', or perhaps something else. There were a zillion fancy names that the makers could have thought of. Why add '*vinglish*' and call it *English Vinglish*? While native English speakers may struggle to understand the addition of 'vinglish', it seems quite natural for us to do it, am I right?

Well, this choice certainly seems influenced by our habit of using certain pairs of words, of which the second word starts with 'व' (pronounced *vuh*) or 'श' (pronounced *shuh*) in Hindi, or with 'ब' (pronounced *buh*) in Marathi.

That is perhaps why we hear a lot of 'चाय वाय (*chai vai*)', 'चाय शाय (chai *shai*)', 'प्यार व्यार (*pyaar vyaar*)', 'खाना वाना (*khaana vaanaa*)', or even 'English vinglish' around us all the time. Grammar Nazis would call it reduplication, which is simply the process in which the root or stem of a word, or a part or whole of it, is repeated exactly or with a slight change.

Reduplications help us sound casual and also do away with the urge to say 'et cetera'. That is why when someone casually asks you 'चाय वाय हो जाए (chai vai *ho jaye*)', they mean to ask if you want to have some tea along with some other drinks, or along with some snacks.

English has its fair share of reduplications too. Baby-shmaby, fancy-shmancy (shm-reduplication); chit-chat, criss-cross (ablaut reduplication); bye-bye, pee-pee (exact reduplication); super-duper, teenie-weenie (rhyming reduplication); and many more.

Since English does have a similar system, you might wonder what the problem could possibly be, if we were to use reduplications when speaking in Indian languages. The answer is quite simple actually.

Firstly, reduplications are used only rarely in English. So, their frequent use itself might raise a few eyebrows. More importantly, the way words are reduplicated in English is very different from how they are reduplicated in Indian languages. Therefore, reduplicating English words the way we do it in our mother tongues is a bad idea, especially in front of a non-Indian audience. As is the case with most Indianisms, you might not be understood, could be misunderstood, or might simply stand out for all the wrong reasons if you use them when speaking to a native speaker of English.

## 27

## Give Me a Break(up)

Every time someone asks me for a 'break-up' after the submission of a quotation or financial proposal, I feel an intense urge to poke some fun at them by asking, 'But when were we in a relationship in the first place?' Fortunately, better sense has always prevailed, and I have never really acted on my desires. But this book is a good medium to rant about it. So, here goes.

You see, in India, it is very common to find people use the noun 'break-up' instead of the noun 'breakdown', when these two actually have very different meanings. A 'break-up' (written as 'break up' when used as a verb) is the end of a relationship, whereas a 'breakdown' (written as 'break down' when used as a verb) is a mechanical failure, the chemical or physical decomposition of something, or the failure of a system.

So, vendor managers should be asking us for a detailed 'breakdown' (an explanatory analysis) of the cost, because a 'break-up' is when couples or even friends separate, or when something is broken into pieces or sections.

The noun 'breakdown' also has other connotations, like there can be a breakdown in a factory or food can be broken down into glucose during digestion, or one can also have a mental, emotional or physical breakdown.

Speaking of a health breakdown, here are some facts about the verb 'break' that you might find useful. When people get well after having come down with a fever, you will hear them say anything from 'I do not have temperature anymore' or 'my temperature is gone', to 'I don't have fever anymore'.

Well, if you 'do not have temperature' or if 'your temperature is gone', you are probably dead. If you are alive and you 'do not have fever anymore', then the right way to say it in English would be 'my fever broke'.

Here is a quick recap:

*'I broke down after my break-up, only to come down with a high fever that eventually broke.'*

There! You have all the words we discussed, together in a sentence for you to see how they are used.

# 28

# Divorced or Still Together?

'Should we be sweet enough and let the words stay together or be the cruel ones to separate the two love birds?'
'Do the words mean the same when they are together as when they stand separated?'
'Can these words be used interchangeably?'
'Does it even make a difference how we write the words?'

These are some of the questions that might haunt you when you look closely at certain English words.

Take the case of 'anyone' and 'everyone'. Or, wait a minute, is it 'any one' and 'every one'? Well, both are correct actually. It is just that they mean different things. 'Anyone' is a pronoun and means 'absolutely any person'; for example:

*<u>Anyone</u> can earn money.*

However, 'any one' is an adjective phrase and means 'any single person (of the possible many ones)'; for example:

*'Employees are allowed up to 21 holidays that can be used in <u>any one</u> of the 12 months.'*

By the way, 'everyone' and 'every one' work according to this exact logic.

But here comes the twist. While most of the time you

*Divorced or Still Together?*

risk making a grammatical mistake when you do not follow the rule, there are times when you can make one by choosing to follow it. That is the problem with English, isn't it? More exceptions than rules, like the haters love to say.

That is exactly the case with 'would not', 'could not' and 'will not'. We always write them separately as per the rule. However, if you decide to follow the rule and write 'can' and 'not' separately, that is suddenly not quite right. That is because 'cannot', unlike the others, is always written as one word. The exception is when 'not' forms part of another construction, for example:

*'War can <u>not only</u> jeopardise relations between nations <u>but also</u> make them poorer.'*

In this above sentence, the 'not' has nothing to do with the 'can', as it is part of the 'not only–but also' construction.

I cannot help but end with this summary sentence that comes to mind. One cannot write the word 'cannot' as 'can not' unless 'can' and 'not' are parts of another construction. I hope the grammar is now clear to everyone so that every one of us avoids these mistakes.

---

### 'Cowlick'

A strange name for sure, but this is the word you would be looking for, to refer to that spiral spot on your head. Yes, the one where the direction of hair growth forms a pattern by virtue of growing at an angle that is at odds with the angle in which the rest of your hair grows.

# 29

# Eat All You Can Drink

A couple of decades ago when we were in London to attend a conference, my colleague and I were out dining with David, one of our regular clients. We had ordered soup and were contemplating what to eat next. When I asked David what he wanted, he said:

*'I think I am going to first finish <u>eating my soup</u> and then decide.'*

I remember my colleague and I sharing a knowing chuckle. David was as British as one could get. How could he, of all people, say 'eat soup'? I remember we had simply put it down to the fact that even native English speakers make mistakes. However, years later, it dawned on us that the joke was actually on us. In English, one does indeed use the verb–noun collocation 'eat–soup'.

If that sounds absurd, let me tell you that closer home, even Bengalis do that. They eat a lot of seemingly drinkable things. And it is not just the water (*jol khabo*; literally, Bengali for 'eat water') or the tea (*cha khabo*; literally, Bengali for 'eat tea') that they eat, they even eat cigarettes! I am sure they have some logic behind why these things are 'eaten' and not 'drunk' or 'smoked' (in case of cigarettes), but let us see why English speakers use such a collocation.

Well, if they need a spoon to consume the soup because it is very thick, then the English would say that they are eating the soup, much like we would say we ate (and not drank) the gravy or the ketchup. That being said, you can 'drink' soups when they are more liquid in nature (clear soups), or when using a mug to consume them. But the generally acceptable usage is to 'eat' soup.

That is how linguistic logic works, I guess; to each their own. Nonetheless, this should serve as useful information to help soup up your culinary English. Happy speaking and happy eating!

## 30

# From Side to Side

There you are, standing with the poise of a flamingo, one leg crushing someone's toe and the other suspended in thin air. Balancing isn't too hard, crammed that you are between several sweaty men. Breathing, however, is hard. So, you point your nose up north, just to avoid choking on the many fetid armpits that surround you. Local trains in Mumbai can be quite unforgiving!

As you continue to balance and breathe somehow, your precarious position is challenged by the impending arrival of the next station. A mass of men begins to move fluidly towards the door. You realise you are being transported too. Not wanting to get off, you try to hold fort, and almost immediately, cries of 'side please' start filling the air.

'Side please' is a creatively Indian way of getting people to clear the way, the meaning of which would unfortunately be lost on most foreigners. Native English speakers would simply go with the informal yet equally effective 'excuse me', or the more formal 'could you move aside, please?'

Speaking of moving things out of our way, is it not surprising that for a nation that is crazy about cricket, we have not even got the terminology right? I have met tons of people who have always believed that the screen that every batsman gesticulates at, while they adjust their groin guards and do those half squats, is a 'side screen'. Turns out, it is called a 'sight screen'. Pretty logical, considering it is meant to ensure that the batsman 'sights' the ball better.

And if you thought that a lot of Indians are confused about 'side' and 'sight', an even greater number are clueless about the difference between the 'back side' and the 'rear'. For us, the 'back side' is usually of things, whereas that would informally just mean 'buttocks' to a native speaker. No wonder we have parking space at the 'back side' of buildings, but native speakers always have it at the 'rear'.

And while we are busting myths, you might want to know that 'sidey characters' and 'sidey people', too, exist only in Indian English. What we call 'sidey' is simply 'shady' or 'creepy' to the native speaker.

So, whether you are a thrilled-to-be-on-TV kind of a debater, a can't-wait-to-jump-in bystander, or simply a have-opinion-will-voice kind of an armchair activist, feel free to take sides, but not before you have made sure that you are on the right side of English grammar.

# 31

## Going Out(side)

When I started my company back in 1993, mobile phones were yet to become India's reality. With only landlines to fall back on, missing important calls was always a possibility. It was at this critical time that Sunita, our in-house Marathi translator, kindly offered to answer calls in my absence. And then one day, when I was out for a meeting, a client happened to call.

When he asked to speak to me, Sunita told him, 'Sorry, but Sandeep has gone outside.'

'No problem. I will hold. Can you please call him inside?' he requested.

'No, I mean he has gone outside to meet a client,' she tried to explain.

'Oh! You mean he has gone out?' the client attempted to confirm, relieved to have finally understood what she was trying to say.

I remember this incident every time I hear someone use the words 'outside' and 'out' interchangeably (something that is fairly common in Indian English). When you are 'outside', you are not in the confines of some space or an enclosed area and can therefore be called 'inside' (to take a call, for example). However, when you have gone 'out', you are not 'in' or present at your home or office.

Interestingly, though, if you are 'going out with someone' that means you are in a regular romantic or sexual relationship with someone. Clearly, to be able to 'go out' with someone, you first need to 'ask the person out'. 'To ask someone out' means to invite someone out on a date. And that is where Indian English has another peculiar idiosyncrasy. Let's have a look.

*'You know, he proposed to her!'*

To a lot of Indians, this sentence would simply mean that some guy asked some girl to be his girlfriend. Perhaps it is the limitation of our English or the variance of our culture that we do not take this to mean anything more. To native English speakers, however, 'to propose' has only one meaning in such a context. It means to ask your partner to marry you.

This would also be a good time to end the 'marriage' and 'wedding' confusion once and for all. No, they are not synonyms. While a 'marriage' simply refers to the relationship between a husband and a wife, or to the state of being married, a 'wedding' is actually the ceremony that gets you married. This means that although you can attend someone's 'wedding' and celebrate, say, 25 years of them 'being married', you cannot possibly attend someone's 'marriage' or celebrate 25 years of their 'wedding'.

Speaking of marriages, they are such a big deal in India! And why wouldn't they be? We can barely wait to get our children married. For a large number of Indians, education is still something that girls are 'allowed to indulge in' while they wait to be married off. With marriages being that central to our society, related advertisements become a necessary evil. Most newspapers even have entire sections devoted to what are called 'matrimonials'.

It is very strange though! So much buzz around a word that does not even exist and that we managed to create out of thin air. Yes, you read that right. The word that practically every mainstream English newspaper in India uses is not even a known word. You have the adjective 'matrimonial' that refers to anything related to marriage or married people. But to create a noun out of it by suffixing a 's' is to technically cross the linguistic line.

There is little chance 'matrimonials' would be understood outside the Indian subcontinent. What we refer to as 'matrimonials', native speakers would simply call 'matrimonial advertisements'.

And unless you are feeling particularly chatty, do not even bother to bring up 'arranged' or 'love' marriages when speaking to people outside Asia. But if it does slip out inadvertently, be a darling and do launch into an explanation about what that means and how and why we marry this way. For those coming from cultures where people only marry out of love, 'arranged marriages' almost look like confessions of being married despite not being in love.

So, do get married by all means. It is our national pastime after all! Do also woo the one you love, ask them out or propose to them, but just make sure you get the terminology right.

# 32

## Fill It Up!

Let's say you want to sign up for a gym membership. You go to the reception counter of a certain gym and make the necessary enquiries. After exhausting all the questions in your quiver, you finally seem to sport a satisfied smile on your face, with perhaps the hope of well-defined abs kindled in your mind. Seeing their chance at closing a sale, the receptionist hands you a form.

Almost anywhere in India, what you would expect to hear after that would be something as predictable as:

*'Sir, please <u>fill</u> this form.'*

Or,

*'Sir, please <u>fill up</u> this form.'*

Not much wrong there to most Indian eyes, right? And why would there be? After all, we do say it in most Indian languages too. Here are some examples:

फ़ॉर्म भरना (form *bharnaa*; literally, Hindi for 'to fill form')

ಫಾರ್ಮ್ ತುಂಬಿಸು (form *tumbisu*; literally, Kannada for 'to fill form')

But obviously, it's not right in English. The right way to say this in English would be:

*'Sir, please fill in this form.'* (British English)

Or,

*'Sir, please fill out this form.'* (American English)

Let's quickly take a look at the difference between 'to fill' and 'to fill in/out', and then also explore a couple of other nuances while on the topic.

'To fill' simply means to cause a container or space to become full or almost full; for example:

*'The hall was filled with people.'*

On the contrary, 'to fill in/out' refers to adding information in order to complete an official form or document. Fits perfectly with what we want to say, doesn't it? This is how it is used:

*'Sir, please fill in/out this form.'*

Then, there is also 'to fill up' which is totally different from 'to fill in/out'. It means to make something completely full, such that there is no more place left. This is how it is used:

*'I filled up the glass with water.'*

And we also have 'to fill in for', which means to act as a substitute for someone when they are unable to do their job. This is how it is used:

*'The class teacher filled in for the history teacher, who was sick.'*

Interestingly, by using the preposition 'on' instead of 'for' after 'to fill in', the meaning changes to letting someone know a missing piece of information. This is how it is used:

*'When my colleague resumed work after a short break, I <u>filled him in on</u> what he had missed while he was away.'*

I think I have had my fill of information. I will now go fill myself a glass of water to sip on, while I fill in this gym membership form that has been lying on my desk ever since I made my New Year's resolution.

---

### 'Crib'

Although it might look like that to us, 'cribbing' does not mean 'to grumble' to a native speaker of English. To them 'to crib' simply means to copy or to steal. Even archaically, it meant to restrain; nothing that ever came close to meaning 'to grumble'. Why not simply say 'grumble' instead of 'crib' then?

# 33

## Giving or Taking?

Why do we Indians love to give things that we should actually be taking, and then sometimes take things that we should be giving? Where do we pick up these incorrect verb–noun collocations, and can we not do something to avoid such mistakes?

Well, a little probing will tell you that a lot of the mistakes we make when we speak English is because we tend to be influenced by our mother tongues. In Marathi, as I am sure is the case with some other Indian languages too, you will find people saying:

मी परिक्षा दिली (*mi pareekshaa dili*; literally, Marathi for 'I gave the exam')

The 'दिली (dili)' then finds its way into our English sentence in the form of 'gave'.

We say 'I will soon be giving an exam' in the sense of 'I have an exam coming up sometime soon'. However, to a native speaker of English, it would mean something very different. 'To give an exam' means that you are going to administer or conduct a test for your students. It does not mean that you are the one who will be appearing for an exam.

It's the same thing when it comes to the word 'tuition'. In Marathi, you will hear teachers say:

मी ट्यूशन घेतो (*mi tuition gheto*; literally, Marathi for 'I take tuition')

*Giving or Taking?*

The 'घेतो (gheto)' then finds its way into our English sentence in the form of 'take'.

We say 'I take French tuitions' in the sense of 'I teach French'. However, to a native speaker of English, it would mean quite the opposite. It would mean that you are learning French.

Simplified, this is what you should be saying:

*'I take an exam'* (when you are writing an exam)
*'I give an exam'* (when you are conducting an exam)
*'I take tuitions'* (when you are learning)
*'I give tuitions'* (when you are teaching)

And by the way, 'tuition' is an uncountable noun and is always used in the singular. Using the plural (tuition<u>s</u>) is again something we tend to do in Indian English. It can be very amusing for people in the English-speaking world.

And then there is also this thing with the word 'studies'. Take for example:

*'I am sorry I will not be able to join you guys for the movie. Siddharth has exams. I need to take his studies.'*

You can get away with making a statement like this practically anywhere in India. Not an eyebrow will be raised, no one will find anything unusual about what you said, or question whether or not this is how it is said in English. Your message will have been conveyed without anyone batting an eyelid.

However, the sentence 'I need to <u>take his studies</u>' is grammatically incorrect. In English, studies cannot be given or taken. Instead, you '<u>help</u> someone study', '<u>help</u> someone with their homework', or '<u>help</u> someone prepare for their exams'.

The easiest way to improve your English, no matter how good it already is, is to constantly check whether you are speaking it the way it is spoken by the native speakers. That way, you will not end up subconsciously translating from one of the Indian languages you speak.

But how will you get access to proper English? Well, it is just a click away. Today, there is no dearth of British and American content on television and on the Internet. British or American news channels, soap operas, films and even podcasts are your best bets.

The more you listen to authentic English, the more you will see the difference between how we say things as opposed to how they are actually said. Once you spot the difference, bringing that into the way you speak is only a matter of persistent usage.

# 34

## I, Me, Myself

The 9/11 attacks introduced us to the concept of 'ground zero', much like the Covid-19 pandemic introduced us to 'patient zero'. Borrowing from these, I would love to find out who the 'culprit zero' in India was when it came to using the pronoun 'myself'. The confidence with which some people use it when introducing themselves can nearly convince the grammatically faint-hearted that it is indeed the right word to use.

Imagine meeting a suave gentleman at a party. You hold out your hand for him to shake, and introduce yourself. And then suddenly, all that style looks like a lie because you hear an American-accented 'hey' followed by a loud and clear 'myself Aditya'. This sounds so horribly wrong that you might as well speak in your mother tongue! Absolutely no shame in doing that, of course. But if you are choosing to speak in English, then you better say it right—and 'myself' does not quite make the cut.

It is, in fact, a classic Indianism that has even been used by stand-up comedians to mock us. Grammatically speaking, 'myself' is a reflexive and intensive pronoun. Being a reflexive pronoun, its action has to reflect back on the pronoun used earlier in the sentence. It cannot simply be used all by itself.

If this is getting too grammatical for your liking, here is a simple way to know if using 'myself' in a sentence is going to be grammatically correct. Check if the pronoun 'I' has already been used earlier in that sentence. If it has been, then you can use 'myself'. For example, check this sentence out:

*'I did it myself.'*

However, when someone says something like 'myself Aditya', it clearly breaches this rule of thumb. Even a sentence like this is wrong:

*'Nobody turned up for the party. It was just Rohan and myself.'*

There is no 'I' used earlier in the sentence and hence using 'myself' would be incorrect.

'Myself' also happens to be an intensive pronoun. This means that its job is to intensify or lay stress on the pronoun it refers back to. For example:

*'You yourself said that it was not true.'*

This sentence intensifies or lays more stress on the pronoun 'you'. Without 'yourself', the word 'you' lacks emphasis in the sentence; for example:

*'You said that it was not true.'*

Long story short, do not use 'myself' in a sentence unless the pronoun 'I' has been used earlier in that sentence. As far as introducing yourself is concerned, a simple 'my name is...' or 'I am...' works just fine.

# 35

## Full Stops, Abbreviations and More

Sometimes, I get the feeling that some people think of their names as sentences and not merely as names. I mean, why else would anyone use a punctuation mark after writing their name or surname? Unless, of course, they are unaware of the rules and are only trying to be safe than sorry.

You will find people signing off letters and emails in this manner every now and then:

*'Best regards,*
*Sandeep Nulkar.'*

Now, this is what we could call a grammatical faux pas. Note the full stop after my name in the example above. The Queen's English (or rather the King's English now, I suppose) allows the use of a full stop only at the end of a sentence or an abbreviation. No question of using one after our names then, since names are neither sentences nor abbreviations. And just so we are clear about what abbreviations are, here is a bird's-eye view of the different kinds of abbreviations—acronyms, contractions, initialisms and shortenings.

Acronyms are words formed from the initial letters of a series of words. They are pronounced as they are spelt and not as separate letters. For example:

*AIDS* (Acquired Immune Deficiency Syndrome)
*SIM* (Subscriber Identification Module) *card*

Contractions, on the other hand, are a type of abbreviation in which letters from the middle of the word are omitted. For example:

*Dr* (Doctor)
*Ltd* (Limited)

You do not need to use a full stop at the end of contractions, as the last letter of the original word is still present. So, technically speaking, you should be writing 'Mr Sandeep Nulkar' and not 'Mr. Sandeep Nulkar'.

Then, you also have initialisms that are abbreviations consisting of the initial letters of each of the words present. They are pronounced as separate letters when they are spoken. For example:

*UK* (United Kingdom; pronounced as *yu-kay*)
*BBC* (British Broadcasting Corporation; pronounced as *bee-bee-cee*)

A full stop is not required after the letters in an initialism. In American English, however, certain initialisms may include full stops if that is the preferred style. For example, 'US' and 'U.S.' are both correct when referring to the United States, as long as you use them consistently across the text.

And finally, we have shortenings that are abbreviations in which the beginning or end of the word has been dropped. In some cases, both the beginning and the end are dropped. For example:

*Flu* (influenza; beginning and end are dropped)
*Ad* (advertisement; middle and end are dropped)

You do not need to use a full stop in a shortening unless it is created specifically for use in writing; for example:

*etc.* (et cetera)

So, where does the word 'short form' fit in all this? Nowhere really. It is a legitimate word only in Indian English. Native speakers will not quite get it. When we say 'short form', we are (unknowingly) only referring to some kind of an abbreviation.

## 36

## Googled, Xeroxed and More

Imagine this scene in some office in India. The boss is very pissed and is seen shouting at his subordinate.

'What the hell have you been doing all this while? Why have you not "bitsed" this document yet?' she says.

Wow! What a day that will be, when people start using 'BITS' (the name of the translation company I founded) as a verb that means 'to translate'. Any marketing guy worth their salt will tell you that when people begin using trademarks as verbs (genericised trademarks), that is a clear sign of how successful the brand has become. Just look around and you will find enough examples.

Don't we all 'Google' (and not 'search on the Internet') in an effort to find the nearest restaurant, look desperately for a place to get our documents 'Xeroxed' (and not 'photocopied'), ask for a 'Bisleri' (and not 'a bottle of mineral water') to quench our thirst, 'FaceTime' (and not 'video call') our friends, 'Bubble Wrap' (and not 'pack with air-cushioned transparent plastic material') gifts, and use a 'Band-aid' (and not an 'adhesive bandage') when we get hurt?

As much as we might identify with such usage, the fact remains that all of these are actually brand names, registered trademarks even. You can use them informally when speaking. Even native speakers of English do. However, if the setting is formal or if there is a need to write it, it is best to refrain from using these. In written, formal communication, their usage is grammatically incorrect.

Let us always use the right verbs and nouns! Using slang or such grammatically incorrect terminology might simply be misconstrued as the inadequacy of our language.

---

### 'Daughter-in-laws'

Common sense might suggest that we need to add an 's' at the end to make it a plural noun. But then, that would be a sign of a lack of grammatical sense. That is because, in this case, 'in-law' is not the noun (although by itself it can be), and is only a modifier. The noun here is 'daughter' and that is what needs to be in the plural form. So, daughters-in-law, please.

## 37

# High Maintenance

To my mind, Sridevi in *Judaai* and Bindu in most movies were the quintessential high-maintenance wives. No one made materialistic look as glamorous as they did, with their lavish kitty parties (and I am surely coming back to this term a little later), fancy clothes, expensive jewellery and, you know, the works.

It was probably the influence of characters like these, coupled with the growing popularity of high-fidelity audio systems during that era, that the word 'hi-fi' came to be associated with human beings. We are probably the only country on the planet to do that.

And look at the range of meanings we have attributed to this concocted word. To us, a 'hi-fi' person is an impressive person, who is either elite or rich or fashionable or classy or high profile or even ultra-intelligent. It is fairly common to hear people talk about a family and say something like:

*'They are hi-fi people.'*

Obviously, not only is this grammatically wrong, it also has no scientific logic to support its usage in such a context. 'Hi-fi' simply means relating to the reproduction of music or other sound with high fidelity. As you can see, it does not have any of the meanings that we have assigned to it.

So, it is best we keep it simple and call people or families rich or elite, or whatever they might be. But let us not call anyone 'hi-fi'.

And just so that there is no confusion, 'hi-fi' is not the same as 'high five', although you will find loads of people pronounce 'five' as 'fi'. When you give someone a 'high five', you want to greet them or celebrate something with them, and hence, you slap the palm of their raised arm with your own.

As for 'kitty parties', although we have a lot of those in India, the concept is alien to the West. They do not have a cultural parallel and that is why the English language does not even have a word for it. A 'tea party' comes close but still misses out on the cultural and monetary undertones.

Sometimes, it is good to be aware of the words that exist only in Indian English. They act as great conversation starters when speaking to foreigners.

# 38

## Hilarious? Not Quite!

So, tell me! What is the opposite of Naag Punchami? Well, it is '*Naag*, do not punch me!' I have one more. Guess what song this would be: 12.9999999? Ha, ha! It is '*Tera, honay lagaa hoon*'. (Non-Hindi speakers may skip these jokes. The point I am trying to make should still make sense.)

I know, I know. These are like the worst 'PJs' I could have probably ever told you. But don't we all have that one friend who can't stop narrating jokes—and silly ones at that? None of them really make us laugh, but nearly all of them make us cringe at the juvenility of the humour. That is perhaps why they came to be known as PJs.

But do you know what the real PJ is? Well, it is that there is no such thing as a 'PJ' or a 'poor joke' or a 'personal joke'. Yes, that is right. We invented it! Funnily enough, the initialism 'PJ' does exist in informal usage. But if you say that to a native speaker of English, they are probably going to be staring at you with a blank expression. For them, a 'PJ' is short for 'pyjamas'—yes, those loose-fitting trousers you sleep in.

So, what do native speakers call a 'poor joke' then? Well, they simply call them 'bad jokes' or 'terrible jokes'.

And by the way, do not confuse a 'practical joke' for a joke. It is not one. It simply refers to a trick played on someone to make them look foolish and to amuse others.

Here is some more trivia about jokes. I am sure you have also heard or said something like 'jokes apart'. Well, that is also an Indianism we seem to have invented. Native speakers say 'joking apart' when they want to indicate that they are now being serious, especially after making a joke.

## 39

# Gone Too Soon

Have you noticed that we Indians are pretty restrained when it comes to using the verb 'to die' when speaking in our mother tongues? It is almost as if using the actual verb to announce the news would seem crude in our culture. It is perhaps for this reason that we will often come across something like this when we speak English:

*'Say not in grief that he is no more but live in thankfulness that he was.'*

Or,

*'Our beloved father left for his heavenly abode.'*

The first one is a popular death and funeral quote, and the second one is how nearly every obituary in practically every Indian newspaper reads. We will come back to these a little later in the chapter. I just thought it would be nice to put these out right in the beginning, to set the tone for what is to follow.

In India, you can easily expect someone to walk out of the intensive care unit, or ICU, of a hospital and announce to the relatives waiting outside, 'Dadaji is no more'. And why just in our private lives, this is something you will also read in Indian newspapers and hear on national television when popular personalities pass away.

But try walking up to a native speaker of English and saying 'John is no more'. I can almost assure you that they would have an inquisitive look on their face expecting you to say something to complete the sentence. Perhaps something like:

*'John is no more than a sentimental fool.'*

Or,

*'John is no more interested in men than he is in women.'*

Even if we presume that there is some context to such a sentence—say that John was in the hospital because he had suffered a heart attack—a native speaker of English would still find the sentence to be a little out of place. That is because native speakers do not use 'no more' in the sense of 'is dead' or 'passed away'.

So, where did we pick this up from? We were probably inspired by the Hindi 'वह अब नहीं रहे (*Veh ab nahi rahay*)', or the Gujarati 'એ હવે રહ્યા નથી (*Ae havay rahaya nathi*)', both literally meaning 'he now is no more'. As right as that might sound in Hindi or Gujarati, or in some other Indian languages, in English one simply says:

*'He died this morning.'*

Or,

*'He passed away last week.'*

Now, coming back to the quote and the obituary, like I said I would. Well, the only reason one can get away with saying 'he is no more' is because this quote is actually from a poem. One, therefore, has the poetic licence to be dramatic. Nothing wrong there!

However, using 'no more' to announce a death is best avoided, especially because it might be mistaken for a bad sense of humour and might land you in awkward situations.

As for the obituary bit, there is an Indianism hiding in plain sight. 'Heavenly abodes' exist only in Indian English. We probably got the idea from the several Indian languages spoken around us that have the concept of a 'heavenly abode', like the Hindi 'स्वर्गवास (*swarg vaas*; literally, "residence in heaven")' or the Punjabi 'ਗੁਰਪੁਰੀ ਵਾਸੀ (*goorpoori vaasi*; literally, "resident of the residence of God")'.

But now that you have read this chapter, it is safe to say that 'heavenly abodes' no longer exist. They are 'no more'!

# 40

# I Will Go. I Will Come Back.

Indian languages are a work of art. No, I mean, really! How many languages would actually allow you to use two verbs, meaning two completely opposite things, and still make perfect sense? Confused, right? Take a look at these examples:

जरा बाहर होके आता हूँ *(jaraa baahar hokay aataa hoon;* literally, Hindi for 'will go out for a bit and come back')

जरा बाहेर जाऊन येतो *(jaraa baaher jaoon yeto;* literally, Marathi for 'will go out for a bit and come back')

Both sentences use multiple verbs with opposite meanings. While one verb 'बाहर होके (baahar hokay)' has the sense of going out, the other one 'आता हूँ (aataa hoon)' is used in the sense of coming back.

So, what's the problem then? Well, none whatsoever, as long as you stick to speaking in an Indian language that allows you the luxury of such a usage. The problem, however, arises when this mother-tongue influence carries over to the English we speak. Very often, you will hear people say:

*'I will quickly go and come.'*

A certain Indian can also be found asking on TripAdvisor if he 'can go to Nainital and come back the same day'. Clearly, this isn't the right way to say it. These sentences would be better constructed thus:

*'I am going to the bakery. I will be back in 20 minutes.'* (Not *'I will go to the bakery and come back in 20 minutes.'*)

Or,

*'Will Nainital be a day's trip?'* (Not *'Can I go to Nainital and come back the same day?'*)

And by the way, did you know that if you are standing in a queue to buy tickets, your 'number does not come' ('numbers' tend to 'come' a lot in Indian English). Rather, if you are standing in a queue, then at some point it is simply 'your turn at the counter'.

*'Alles klar? Wunderbar!'* as they say in German, meaning 'All clear? Wonderful!'

---

### 'Denims'

Although that is what we call a pair of jeans, denims need not always refer to jeans. 'Denims' is a generic way of referring to any garment that is made of denim. To summarise, denim is the material, while a pair of jeans are the trousers that are made of denim.

# 41

## Job Hunting

I have always been amused by some of the job applications we have received over the years. We once received an application from a 'sweetpinky87@xxx.yyy'. Since I could not have cared less whether Pinky was sweet or not, I quickly saw through how she had tried to butter me up with the usual 'would be an honour to work with your esteemed company' and went on to open the CV she had said was attached to the mail. To my surprise, however, when I opened the CV, it was called a 'bio-data'.

Sweet Pinky's CV was probably inspired by an equally sweet and helpful friend, who must have found the word 'bio-data' to be a better option. I have also seen other options being used by potential candidates, be it the more common 'résumé' or the rare '(career) profile'. I get the feeling that people think these nouns have identical meanings and that they are free to pick one, depending on what they find smarter or more elegant. Unfortunately, it does not work that way. So, let us start with the basics.

A résumé (do not forget those accents) is the most basic one. It is a very brief summary of your educational qualifications, skill sets and work experience. It is intended to give potential employers a quick idea of what a cool person you are. So, do not torture them by dumping all kinds of information on their already-clogged brains. A résumé should be no more than a page in length; two at the very most.

A CV, short for curriculum vitae, is where you can brag a little bit more. A CV would typically be between three and four pages in length and can have a slightly longer summary of your educational qualifications, skill sets and work experience. A CV can also talk about your employment history, any awards or honours that you might have received, any publications against your name, and a little about your interests.

A biodata (and not 'bio-data') is perhaps one of the most incorrectly used words in Indian English. Used rampantly as a replacement for words like 'résumé' and 'CV', it has technically got nothing to do with job hunting. 'Biodata' is short for 'biographical data' and is a term related to industrial and organisational psychology.

Used in a colloquial context, a biodata usually provides a lot more information about a person and includes details such as personal information, physical attributes, interests, hobbies and even a photo at times. It is something you would draft or have for matrimonial or even medical reasons.

A '(career) profile' is, well, nothing. It is just a fancy word someone chose to use because 'résumé' or 'CV' did not sound upmarket enough. If you are looking for a job, a CV is what you will need, unless someone specially asks for your résumé.

No matter what you send out, just make sure to call it by the right name, and while you are at it, also send it from a professional-sounding email address. You surely do not want to be remembered like our 'sweetpinky87'!

## 42

## Keep It Back

What is the problem with Indian English? What is wrong if we speak it with pride and expect the world to accept it as a legitimate dialect? I am asked these questions very often. The English-speaking population of our country is much larger than the population of countries where English is the first language.

Well, language is not only about communicating or being understood. It is also about connecting with people and being relevant, and dialects help you connect and resonate way better than just the language. So, Indian English works perfectly well when two Indians are speaking. We could not care less how things are said as long as we understand each other.

But hey, are we not supposedly living in a globalised world of ever-shrinking borders? We are not always going to be conversing just with Indians, and that is where neutral English, English free of all Indianisms, becomes extremely important. What's more, native speakers of English have an extremely simple way to say complex things. And complicating things can also be a form of Indianism.

Take, for instance, the following sign at my gym. It is the perfect example of how we complicate things. For me, it was all the more striking because I had seen this exact message being conveyed at a gym in London, but way more effortlessly. The sign at my gym in India read:

*'You are requested to keep <u>all the weights and other equipment</u> back in their proper places after use.'*

And this is what I remember reading at the gym in London:

*'Please <u>replace</u> all equipment after use.'*

You see, we do not seem to realise that the weights we lift also qualify as 'equipment'. Using both, 'weight' and 'equipment', is therefore unnecessary. Then, most Indians have a very inadequate understanding of the verb 'to replace'. No one ever told us that, apart from a host of other meanings, 'to replace' also means to put something back in its proper place.

More is not always better. Minimum words, maximum impact! If we keep it short, simple and crisp, it also ensures that we are creating a better impression on the listener.

# 43

# Last Man Standing

Playing cricket and fighting seemed like inseparable bedfellows to us as kids. One never knew when a game would be cut short by a narcissistic neighbour refusing to return the ball, or when, in the middle of a match, a heartless mother would mercilessly summon her offspring, who also happened to own the goddamn bat.

It was perhaps this insecurity, coupled with the desire to play out our cricketing fantasies, that made alpha boys clamour aggressively for the top batting spots. Victory for the meeker ones simply meant not having to bat last. It was around this time that I first remember hearing a nerdy loser claim the 'second last' spot.

The trick was smart, but the word not so much. It is not even a legitimate English word. And yet, I have heard it a zillion times since, from all sorts of people. From rows in auditoriums to rankings in races, a lot of things in our lives can be 'second last'. It is probably safe to avoid this Indianism though.

One can use the phrase 'second to last' (informal) or even the phrase 'last but one' (informal). However, what works best is the adjective 'penultimate' (formal). Here are some examples for you to get an idea of the usage:

*'The teacher asked the student to read the <u>second to last</u> paragraph.'*

*'Our team finished <u>last but one</u> in the relay.'*
*'He will now bowl his <u>penultimate</u> over.'*

So, here is a question for you. If you overtake the last person in a race, what position will you be at in the race? Did you just think 'penultimate'? I am going to leave you to figure this one out. So much for lateral thinking!

# 44

## Lucky Me

Like every year, I was chaperoning the missus from mall to mall. Husbands being emotionally blackmailed to come along on retail odysseys, and the energy in their stride being inversely proportional to the time they have been married, is a common sight during festive seasons in India.

Words like 'discount' and 'cashback' only seemed to prolong the ordeal as my better half walked into anything that even remotely resembled a shop. While wifey dear was looking increasingly happy, I was beginning to attract attention for the disproportionate number of shopping bags I was carrying.

And just when I thought we were done, I found her standing at the entrance of yet another shop. She was looking at this big banner and then she suddenly shrieked, 'Lucky draw!'

I will spare you the rest of the story, but 'lucky draw'? Seriously? It was the first time I was paying so much attention to this word (that is not even an English word actually). It is probably just an example of us coining words.

I mean, it looks like we saw someone drawing something and someone getting lucky, and bam, we decided to call it a 'lucky draw'. Native English speakers call it a 'lucky dip' by the way, and it is called 'grab bag' in American English. Moreover, what a 'lucky draw' means to us and what a 'lucky dip' means to native speakers are quite different things.

To us, a 'lucky draw' entails someone drawing coupons or other proofs of purchase in our absence to decide the winner. Our prizes, too, tend to be as lavish as cars or even all-expenses-paid holidays. However, to a native speaker a 'lucky dip' is simply a game in which small prizes concealed in a container are chosen at random by the participants themselves.

Lucky draw or lucky dip—horses for courses I say. Although 'lucky draw' works perfectly well in India, if you do see an oblivious non-desi walk past the opportunity to win something nice, do explain how the concept works in our country.

---

### 'Doubts'

When an Indian says they have 'doubts', they mean they have not understood something properly, and that they have questions or need clarifications. To a native speaker, 'a doubt' only means a feeling of uncertainty or the lack of conviction. It is best to go with the simple 'I have a couple of questions' or 'I need some clarifications', instead of saying 'I have a doubt'.

## 45

## Lunch in a Box

For the greater part of my teens, the sight of a *dabbawalla* (a person who brings packed lunch to people) riding a cycle loaded with tiffin used to send my gastric juices in overdrive. My brain was wired to think of food each time I saw a tiffin. However, some major rewiring happened in my late 20s when I started touring the south of India on work.

A word that had only meant to me a stainless-steel container carrying delicious meals until then, began assuming newer meanings. I noticed that the word 'tiffin' was rampantly used down south to mean both lunch as well as the place that served it. Tiffin centres were as common as the people who would ask you if you had had your tiffin.

Many years later, my brain stood completely rewired. I learnt that the meaning we attribute to the word 'tiffin' is nothing but a figment of Indian imagination. To the British, a 'tiffin' is simply a cake, or a dessert made with biscuits, syrup and chocolate. Who would have guessed?

As for the container in which food is packed, they simply call it a 'lunch box' ('lunch pail' in American English). Even the words 'tiffin box' and 'tiffin carrier' that are used commonly in India belong to Indian English. To a native speaker, those would still be 'lunch boxes'.

And since a 'tiffin' does not mean a lunch or even a lunch box, saying that you need to 'make' someone's tiffin every morning would be wrong too. One cooks a meal and then packs it as lunch in a lunch box. Simple!

Trace the etymology of the word 'tiffin' and you will find that it comes from the English colloquial term 'tiffling' that means to take a little drink. The word 'tiffin' might have eventually come to be used to indicate the British custom of having tea with some snacks in the afternoon.

A lot of words that are commonly used in Indian English are either archaic in British English, or are ones that have acquired meanings that native speakers do not attribute to them. Learning to identify such words and replacing them with the correct ones would go a long way in improving the comprehensibility and quality of our English.

## 46

## Insistence Unlimited

This happened in Berlin a few years ago, on one of my work trips. Although weekdays are usually a blur, weekends act as the perfect setting to catch up with friends. So, on a particular Saturday evening, I decided to meet up with my friend Hans.

No sooner had we settled down at the table, than the waiter was there to take our order. I was doing the ordering, as I had told Hans that I would be picking up the tab that evening. Trying to be a good host, I asked him what he wanted to drink. I was actually surprised when he said water would be just fine. I knew he liked his beer and it had been a while since we had had one together. The natural Indian instinct in me was to ask if he was sure he didn't want one, and to insist he have at least one 'for old times' sake'. The one-line factual reply he gave me after that was almost like a crash course in cross-cultural adaption.

'But I already said I don't want any beer!' he shot back.

You see, personal space, opinions and choices are sacrosanct in most European cultures. No matter how close people are, those lines are rarely crossed. Although he did not take offence at being asked a second time, his reaction was a reflection of his culture.

Cut to somewhere in India and personal space seems like an illusion, opinions seem like a fallacy, and individual choices are opportunities to ridicule people or gossip about them! In a land where your guest is considered God, we are hardwired to not take our guests' 'no' very seriously and continue to confidently engage with them in a deadly duel of one-upmanship, where guests will eventually cave in under the pressure of our culinary onslaught and eat until they bloat.

Depending on our mother tongues, their influence in English will show up through a variety of verbs. The most common ones that I have heard border on the usual:

'They forced me to eat until I was stuffed.'

Or,

'They made me eat until I was stuffed.'

And sometimes, the not-so-usual:

'They kept serving me even though I was full.'

None of these, however, capture the love with which we feed our guests. They look like heartless actions, carried out nearly at gunpoint. But then, how do you explain this cultural thing we do out of affection to someone whose culture does not have a parallel? What do you say so that they understand you? Insisting that someone eats after they have refused would be a transgression into their personal space, and also disrespecting the choice they have made.

So, back to what you should be doing instead. Obviously, the best thing to do is to respect the 'no'. However, if you are feeling overly hospitable and are in the mood to give your guests a taste of Indian hospitality, here is a cultural tip that will tell you how to communicate this effectively. You can say:

*'Indian hospitality entails feeding you with such love that we might sometimes come across as being overbearing, but trust me, that is only because our idea of having taken care of you is to see that you have wasted at least a little food.'*

This should set the tone for them to not misunderstand the persistent insistence. As for how do you actually say 'they forced me to eat', 'they made me eat' or 'they kept serving even though I didn't want to eat' in better English, you can simply say something like:

*'They fed me with such love-worthy insistence that I was beyond stuffed.'*

Or,

*'Their hospitality left me stuffed.'*

Intercultural communication is a skill for a reason. We cannot always do it our way and get away with it. It is, therefore, prudent to first understand the cultural differences so that we can then figure out the right thing to say or do.

# 47

## Kindly Please

After yet another particularly lengthy business trip, I found myself at one of the boarding gates of the Charles de Gaulle Airport in Paris, waiting to head back to where my heart belonged.

It did not take too long for me to realise, however, that my stay in France had spoilt me rotten! I had seemingly picked up these bad habits that made uncivilised behaviour seem intolerable, and noise seem like a nuisance. That was surprising considering this was like a regular day in India for me. Thankfully, what I was about to experience at the airport prepared me for a lifetime in India.

The sitting area around the boarding gate resembled a mini-India already. It seemed like every Indian living in Paris had suddenly decided to fly back on that very day. Decibel levels were high enough to make it difficult for me to hear my own voice, and the entire area was like an olfactory reminder of the choicest packaged foods of India. Leave alone a place to sit, there was barely enough place to stand.

Luckily, I saw an empty seat to the rightmost end of the last row. I settled into my seat and decided to call my wife and daughter before boarding commenced. Since the ambient noise was making it nearly impossible for me to hear their voices, I simply turned in my seat at a right angle, so as to move slightly away from the noisy gentleman sitting beside me. Mind it, I was still occupying a third of the seat.

A couple of minutes into the conversation, I felt a nudge and before I knew it, I was pushed off my seat! I could not believe that some random guy, who until now was standing in front of my seat, had actually thought it was all right to sit in a seat that I was already sitting in.

Part shocked and part angry, I thundered, 'What do you think you are doing?'

'Sorry, boss! You are talking on the phone anyway. Kindly please adjust a bit,' said the gentleman with stoic shamelessness.

I realised much later, what he had said was as funny as what he had done. No grammatically sensible person will use 'kindly' and 'please' together! Even separately, some people tend to use 'kindly' and 'please' as interchangeable words, which they are not. They mean different things.

'Kindly' is an adverb that tells us how an action is being performed. If I say 'I would like to kindly apologise for any inconvenience caused', it means I am apologising and doing so in a kind manner. As you would agree, we cannot replace 'kindly' with 'please' in this sentence.

Similarly, 'kindly' can also be used to demand something, perhaps even in an ironic sense, for example:

*'Could you kindly explain why you did not show up?'*

There is no sense of a request here and hence one cannot replace 'kindly' with 'please'. That is because 'please' is an adverb used in polite requests or questions, for example:

*'Could you please help me find this place?'*

Or,

*'What is the name of this building, please?'*

In a way, 'kindly' and 'please' are mutually exclusive. Using them in one sentence is therefore grammatically incorrect. Let me now draw your attention to the more interesting part, the part where I was asked to 'adjust'.

Indians are probably the most hospitable people on the planet. From people and customs to languages and words, we have always been very accommodative. It is probably an extension of this nature that allows us to seldom think twice before asking fellow Indians to fit in with our wishes or needs. If we could adjust for invaders and rulers, why not adjust for our own people, seems to be the underlying logic.

And you could be at the receiving end of such requests practically anywhere, from cinema halls and schools to hospitals and crematoriums. And, not so surprisingly, we even have a way to say it in most Indian languages, such as:

थोड़ा adjust करना *(thodaa* adjust *karnaa;* literally, Hindi for 'adjust a little')

ಸ್ವಲ್ಪ ಅಡ್ಜಸ್ಟ್ ಮಾಡಿ (*swalpa* adjust *madi;* literally, Kannada for 'adjust a little')

By the way, it would be ill-advised to engage in such misadventures when travelling outside India. People might not take to such requests too 'kindly'. This surely works, but only in India!

## 48

## Meet and Greet

Did you know that the popular WhatsApp derives its name from the informal American way of greeting people? Americans will ask you 'what's up?' to mean 'what is going on?', or 'how are you?' or even 'hello', depending on the context.

A seemingly simple way of greeting people, but so much of class and generational distinction is hidden in there. The wannabes in India will ape the Americans and ask you 'Wassup?', while a younger millennial might stick to a shortened 'Sup?' The foreign-returned dude will try and drive home his coolness with a 'hey', while those who want to play it safe will go with the simpler 'hi' or 'hello'.

Take your pick but know that these aren't exactly synonyms. There are rules that govern their usage and you do not want to be caught using the wrong one. 'Hi' and 'hello' mean the same but the former is informal whereas the latter is used in more formal situations. 'Hey' is the same as 'hi' and 'hello' but is used only informally and only in the United States (US). 'Wassup' and 'sup' are slang and used mostly by young adults.

And yes, please do not take the pain to add our favourite 'ji' to the 'hello'. It makes it more Indian, not more formal, and certainly not more endearing.

### 'Get Medicines'

Let us get this straight. It is not really possible to 'get medicines' miraculously, you need to go out and buy them. Incidentally, there is a nice little phrase in English to say precisely that. It is 'to refill a prescription' which means to buy another set of doses or medicines as mentioned on a prescription.

# 49

# Nothing to Worry About

Like most Indians, I was oblivious to a grammatical error we have been making for the longest time. It was only in 2004, when one of our British clients sent us feedback on a document that we had translated, that I finally saw how funny it must have been all along for native speakers to hear us use this Indianism.

Our client was referring to this one sentence in that document, translated as:

> *'Any non-compliance must be reported to the concerned authority.'*

The true-blue Brit that he was, our client pointed out that although the quality of our translation was good (always praise before you criticise), he had found the use of the term 'the concerned authority' to be very 'amusing' (British below-the-belt speak for 'stupid').

Had he not gone on to explain what he meant, I would have perhaps never understood what was so wrong about it. 'The concerned person' or 'the concerned authority' is something you will hear in India all the time. Unfortunately, that does not make it grammatically right.

The thing is that there are two types of adjectives—prepositive and postpositive. Simply put, prepositive adjectives are those that are placed before the noun or pronoun they qualify, for example:

*'He was a good (adjective) boy (noun).'*

Postpositive adjectives, on the contrary, are those that are placed after the noun or pronoun they qualify, for example:

*'All matters (noun) legal (adjective) were referred to him.'*

But then, there are also those adjectives that can be both prepositive and postpositive, and their meaning changes depending on where they are placed. Turns out, 'concerned' is one such adjective.

What we actually mean when we say 'we will speak to the concerned person' is that we will speak to the person who is in charge or who is responsible in this matter. However, 'concerned' will mean that only when used as a postpositive adjective (after the noun). When used as a prepositive adjective (before the noun), it simply means 'worried'. No wonder our client found it 'amusing'!

Oh! And yes, whoever thought of saying 'concern person' was way out of grammatical line. 'Concern' is a noun, not an adjective. Time to keep our adjectives in check!

## 50

## Meatily Amusing

Like 'functional fitness', if 'functional language' were to be a thing, Indian English would be a clear winner. No one twists and turns or even invents words to make them mean whatever we want, the way we do. The results are sometimes hilarious, and sometimes disastrous.

Take the case of the words 'vegetarian' and 'non-vegetarian' for example. They are simple words that can be used either as nouns or as adjectives to refer to and differentiate between people who eat or do not eat meat, fish or other animal products.

And fortunately, we do get the usage right. Well, mostly. We are surely on point when we say something like vegetarian (informally, veg) or non-vegetarian (informally, non-veg) delicacies, or call someone a veg or a non-veg person, or even call friends veg or non-veg. However, there are times when we use these words in a way that is not grammatically correct, and yet, that does not stop us.

In Indian English, we actually have jokes that are veg or non-veg! As creative as that might seem, I think that is taking things too far. Native English speakers would simply call them adult jokes, dirty jokes, vulgar jokes or sexy jokes.

But, come to think of it, the idea of 'non-veg jokes' does not sound too illogical, viewed from an Indian perspective. There is a reason why adult jokes might have come to be known as 'non-veg jokes' in India.

You see, two things have predominantly been a taboo in India: talking openly about sex and eating non-vegetarian food. If you put these two together, you will see how they become the perfect raw material for the analogy. Much like non-veg food is the food that you are better off not consuming, non-veg jokes are the ones that you are better off not narrating or listening to.

Now you see why I said we twist and turn words to lend them whatever meaning we want. We can be proud of being able to do so or even be happy with the flexibility of expression that doing this offers us, but let us please not brandish such usage on non-Indians. The poor fellows would have no clue what hit them.

# 51

## Movie Magic

Watching movies used to be such a surreal experience back in the 1980s. Stars were not as overexposed as they are today. Getting the chance to even catch a glimpse of your idol could create mass hysteria. There was devotional yearning when we gaped with dropped jaws at their larger-than-life cut-outs or stared at the screen in rapt attention as they blurted out one overdramatic dialogue after another.

What added to the allure was that a seat in the movie hall was never assured. There were only so many screens in a city and those, too, had a limited number of shows. 'First-day first-show' was a thing and the average enthusiast invariably ended up buying tickets 'in black'. Serpentine queues at ticket counters and insane crowds surrounding every black marketeer were common sights, as were makeshift boards announcing that the show was 'housefull'.

Shows being 'housefull' is such an integral part of our collective experience as a society that we have all been at the receiving end of it at some point. It was therefore a real shocker when I learnt that this word does not even exist in English, and certainly not in the form and sense we use it.

To begin with, 'houseful' is spelt with a single 'l' and cannot be used as an adjective like we do; for example:

*'The show was houseful.'*

'Houseful' means having a lot of people or things in your house and is used as a noun that is usually followed by the preposition 'of', for example:

*'We had a houseful of guests.'*

So, what do native English speakers say when they want to indicate that there are no more movie tickets left to sell? Well, they would say something like:

*'All tickets were sold out.'*

Or,

*'It was a full house.'*

By the way, native speakers do not use or understand the Indian concept of 'first-day first-show'. You will not find this in any English dictionary. If a native speaker has to say something along these lines, they would simply say:

*'I watched the first show of the film on the first day that it was screened.'*

And there is something else that is peculiar about this whole movie business. No, it is not the touts. The touts are a rarity in times when online bookings and multiplexes rule the roost. What I am talking about is buying tickets 'in black'. It is very Indian to say that. In English, stuff is bought 'on the black market'.

Up for a movie tonight then? You can save yourself the trouble and just catch one on Netflix. No chance you would see a 'housefull' board there.

# 52

## Ms Julie

The boss storms into his office, a sense of purpose written all over his face. There is a briskness to his walk that betrays his no-nonsense attitude. Then, as he makes his way from the entrance to his cabin, the dozens of nincompoops that he has employed begin standing up in quick succession, in an attempt to flatter him with a subservient 'good morning'.

Films used to be so melodramatic back in the 1970s and '80s. The boss in question also usually had a stereotypical secretary, whose name always defied the religious diversity of India. I have rarely seen their names go beyond an unimaginative Julie, Lily, Roma, or the like. What was funnier was that no matter how lecherously the boss eyed her, he always made it a point to address her as 'Ms Julie' or 'Ms Lily', in a forced attempt to display some respect.

Now, what does this have to do with Indian English or an Indianism, you might wonder? Quite a bit actually! Even today, as you read this chapter, someone somewhere in India is being called 'Ms Jyoti' or 'Mr Sandeep'. This practice of using a 'Ms' or 'Mr' before the first names of people, and not before their surnames, is in itself very Indian.

Correct usage entails that no matter what title you use—'Ms', 'Mr' or 'Mrs'—it should always be followed by the surname or the full name of the person. For example:

'*Mr Sandeep*' (wrong usage)
'*Mr Sandeep Nulkar*' (correct usage)
'*Mr Nulkar*' (also correct usage)

And yes, the seemingly missing full stop after 'Ms' or 'Mr' is not an oversight. The correct way to write contractions is indeed without the full stop. As mentioned in an earlier chapter, contractions are a type of abbreviation in which only the first and the last letters of a word are retained. So, 'mister' becomes 'Mr', for example. Grammatically speaking, the reason you do not need to use a full stop at the end of contractions is because the last letter of the original word is still present.

I better go now. I am a little low on melodrama, I think. Perhaps I should watch *Zanjeer*. Ajit and Roma would be the perfect antidote!

---

### 'Having Specs'

You will find many people say that they 'have specs'. But that only means that they have bought a pair or have them on their person. 'Having specs' is not the same as needing them. To actually suggest that you cannot read without using spectacles, you must say that you 'need' them.

# 53

## Let It Be!

It is surprising how some verbs can actually have two nearly opposite meanings. Take the case of the verb 'to leave', for example. It means 'to go away' as much as it means 'to allow or to cause to remain'. You see what I mean? 'Go away' and 'remain'—two completely opposing meanings.

But that is not half as funny as how we Indians are able to turn and twist this verb to make it look like the most perfect choice in a diverse number of situations. So, what can Indians 'leave', then? Well, just about anything actually!

Indian cricketers can leave (and not 'drop') catches, while Indian brothers can leave (and not 'drop off') their sisters at the bus stop. You can also ask someone to leave something they are doing (God knows what that even means) so that you can do it yourself, for example:

*'Leave, let me do it.'*

And then, so many of our friends leave (not 'quit') smoking one fine night, only to start puffing on leftover stubs the next morning. An equally high number of Indian hosts insist that guests must leave (not 'save') some place (not 'room') in their stomach for some dessert.

The reason we use the verb 'leave' in so many places is because we are unknowingly translating from our mother tongues, or from the various Indian languages that are spoken around us. I am sure most Indian languages, including Hindi, use the equivalent of the verb 'to leave' in such cases. Have a look at these examples from Hindi:

catch छोड़ना (catch *chowdna*; literally, 'leave catch')

bus stop पर छोड़ना (bus stop *par chowdna*; literally, 'leave at bus stop')

छोड़ ना! मैं करता हूँ! *(Chowd na! Mai kartaa hoon!*; literally, 'Leave it! I will do it!')

cigarette छोड़ना (cigarette *chowdna*; literally, 'leave cigarette')

dessert के लिए जगह छोड़ना (dessert *kay liyay jagaha chowdna*; literally, 'leave place for dessert')

We simply cannot seem to leave the verb 'leave' alone!

The problem here is that we are using a hybrid verb–noun collocation, if I can call it that. By hybrid collocations, I mean collocations that employ a purely English noun but use a verb that has been translated from an Indian language. Such hybrid collocations will always end up amusing or confusing native English speakers.

I have said this often, and I am going to say it again. If I had to put it down to that *one thing* that can make our English look impeccable, it is not our accent or our vocabulary but the quality of the collocations we use. Get them right, and that is when you will begin nailing it!

# 54

# Like How?

Typical pre-wedding scenes in India: 'the boy's side' (and not 'the boy's family') comes over to 'see the girl' (and not 'meet the girl's family'). Some small talk later, the guests settle down. Elaborate sugar- and fat-laden eatables are served. As the eatables are being gobbled down, questions and answers start flying back and forth. The girl and boy are sent away to quickly fall in love with each other. They emerge after a while, and the families seem reasonably happy with the meeting. Some more small talk ensues, and then it's time to leave.

Once the boy's family leaves, the contained excitement is unleashed and one enthusiastic aunt proclaims:

> *'That <u>way if you go to see</u>, he is the perfect choice for Radha!'*

This typical Indianism will not make much sense to a native speaker of English. What 'way' are we talking about and where are we 'going' and what will we 'see'? Too much confusion!

What that aunt probably meant was simply:

> *'I think he is the perfect choice for Radha.'*

Why then did she say 'that way if you go to see'? Well, that is nothing but another example of subconsciously translating from our mother tongues. Look at these examples:

वैसे देखा जाए तो (*waisay dekhaa jayay toh*; literally, Hindi for 'that way if you go to see')

ਓਦਾਂ ਵੇਖਿਆ ਜਾਵੇ ਤਾਂ (*oda vekhiyaa javay taan*; literally, Punjabi for 'if seen like that')

You will find variations of this in most Indian languages.

So, if this is not the right way to say it in English, then how exactly does one say it? Firstly, please consider that you don't have to say something just to be polite or to segue into the main point. Saying what you feel directly without any 'starter' phrase is also a valid option. However, if you feel the urge to say something, starting your sentence with a simple 'well' can suffice.

However, if a topic is being discussed wherein people are expressing two very diverse opinions, then you can also say:

*'Looked at in one way, he is the perfect choice for Radha!'*

This has the sense of 'viewed from one perspective'. And a counter-opinion can be expressed by starting the sentence with 'viewed from the other perspective'.

Today, we all have access to a lot of English movies and shows. It would be a good practice to observe the various ways in which characters start their sentences. Your observations will surely come in handy!

## 55

## Mobile Mania

As ridiculous as it might sound today, mobile phones were once a style statement in our country. The nouveau riche rarely squandered an opportunity to flash their awkwardly bulky device that they, for some reason, chose to constantly hold in their hands (a very Indian habit, by the way). To ensure people did not miss this piece of technological brilliance, they spoke in elevated tones, with the elbow of the hand that held the gadget to their ear usually pointing up.

The coolness quotient was further enhanced by calling their gizmo by different names. While the flamboyant folks preferred the ostentatious 'cell phone', the plebeians went with the simpler 'mobile'. Every yuppy chose to call it a 'cell', while that rare oddball made sure to stand out by calling it a 'cellular phone'. Eventually, 'smartphones' and 'satellite phones' were added to the mix too. All these words might look like synonyms, but in reality they are not.

The word 'mobile phone' ('cell' or 'cell phone' in American English) is actually the grammatically correct term to use. The word 'mobile' is technically an adjective more than it is a noun, although native English speakers do refer to 'mobile phones' as 'mobiles' in day-to-day conversations.

'Smartphones' (also 'feature phones') are phones that make their owners look smart by performing many of the functions of a computer, whereas 'satellite phones' (the ones that Ajmal Kasab and company brought along) are also mobile phones, but ones that use orbiting satellites instead of terrestrial cell sites to connect to a network.

From being an extension of our palms and our sixth finger to becoming our better half, the staggering 1.2 billion+ phones in our country have had every moniker you can imagine. As creatively satisfying as these options may look, let the grammar not be lost on us when it comes to speaking and writing formally.

# 56

## Of(f) and Away

Prepositions have long been the nemesis of many an Indian speaker of English. Using the wrong ones is one type of Indianism. For example, Indians get 'in' a bus instead of getting 'on' it. Then, there is also another type of Indianism, one that occurs from using a preposition when none is needed. This type can be very confusing.

Take the example of the preposition 'of'. It seems to be such a simple little preposition that we have used confidently all our lives. We have always said 'consists of'. For example:

*'This section consists of fifteen chapters.'*

Then one day, for the sake of variety, we may use the verb 'comprise' instead of the verb 'consist', and suddenly, the grammar police find you guilty. Here's why.

The verb 'comprise' actually means 'to be made up of' or 'to consist of'. As you can see, the preposition 'of' is already a part of the meaning and hence it is not necessary to use it again. Some dictionaries would support the use of 'be comprised of' in the passive voice. However, if you wish to ally with the purists, you are advised to stay away from using it, although resistance to its use is weakening in common parlance.

Also, if we are talking about 'of', then we cannot not talk about how people tend to use it after 'off'. Truth be told, using 'off of' is avoidable since it is frowned upon in standard, modern British English. For example:

'*I picked it up off of the floor.*'

The correct way to say it in British English would be:

'*I picked it up off the floor.*'

The Americans, however, have no such qualms.

The Brits and the Americans will always be at loggerheads when it comes to English. It is up to you to decide who you want to go along with. Just make sure you do not mix the two.

---

### 'Insufferable'

Although one could be tempted to believe it does, the word 'insufferable' has got nothing to do with suffering. It actually means something or someone who is intolerable or too extreme to bear. I don't think any examples are needed here. I am sure you know enough people and things that would qualify.

## 57

# On and Off

Did you know that in English there are over a dozen verbs you can use to suggest that you have powered up or powered down a device? Now, imagine the sheer number of tools and gadgets we use in our day-to-day lives, and you will probably begin to understand the scale of the linguistic problem that Indians face. We simply do not know what the right verb to use is!

Do you 'turn' a TV off or do you 'switch' it off? Do you 'turn' a laptop on, or do you simply 'start' it? When we speak in our mother tongues, we seldom face such problems. Having heard enough of the language all around us ever since we were kids (known as linguistic immersion), we have an in-built sense that every native speaker does. We know exactly what verb–noun collocation to use in our mother tongues.

With no such linguistic immersion or heritage to fall back on when it comes to English, it is jungle *raaj* (rule) at its worst. Everyone is free to use a verb of their liking, irrespective of whether it makes any grammatical sense. And that is precisely why customer support executives in India have received complaints like:

*'My screen is not coming on.'*

Or,

*'My screen is not showing anything.'*

Or,

*'My screen is looking all black black.'*

Let me explain the logic so that it becomes easier for you to pick the right verb. Technically speaking, any device that has a knob is usually turned on (or off). That is why you 'turn' the gas stove off. Any device that has a button is usually switched on (or off). That is why you 'switch' off the TV. That being said, it is now common to use these verbs like interchangeable options in daily parlance.

As regards a laptop or a computer, those have hardware as well as software and run on electricity. That is why you can 'power them on (or off)' or 'power them up (or down)', or even 'boot them up (or down)', or then 'start them up' or 'shut them down'.

As for the 'black black' screen that 'is not showing anything' or 'refusing to come on', you can simply say that it is 'acting up'. In fact, you can use this phrasal verb for any gadget or device that fails to function properly.

Now, if you really want to get this right, I suggest you ask yourself what the right verb to use would be every time you find yourself using a gadget. And when in doubt, just turn to this chapter.

## 58

## Out of Thin Air

There are words in English that we pronounce a certain way because we have either never read them carefully enough to realise how they are spelt, or have simply heard people around us pronounce them that way. Moreover, we may have never really bothered to check if that is the right pronunciation because, hey, in India it hardly matters. People understand us anyway.

When I was a teeny-weeny kid, we had a Fiat Millecento that I was in love with. Our lucky gardener was entrusted with the job of washing that Italian beauty every weekend. Not one to keep my hands off it so easily, every time he washed the car, I used to get into the driver's seat and start shadow driving. And when he tried to shoo me away, I used to move into the other seat and start ransacking the 'glowbox'.

That's right! Up until I hit my teens, that is what I thought it was called because our gardener kept asking me not to touch the goddamn 'glowbox'. Eventually, I learnt that it was actually a 'glovebox' and he was just pronouncing it the way he had heard my father say it. The 'glowbox' episode reminds me of the legacy of a few more Indianisms from different walks of life.

My personal favourite is the 'momento', that fancy little object we give out as a souvenir. Many an organiser has been guilty of this pronunciation. Why, I have even seen it written on boards outside shops that make them. Unfortunately, that is neither how it is written nor how it is pronounced. The word is spelt as m-e-m-e-n-t-o, and pronounced as *may-men-to*.

Then there are 'sponsorers', the large-hearted people who fund our events. Many an organiser has also been guilty of thanking 'sponsorers' and not 'sponsors'. Yes, there are nouns one can form by adding the suffix '-er' to verbs. However, some people seem to miss the fact that 'sponsor' is already a noun.

Talking about sponsors and events, there is an Indianism that is very common in athletic events. You will hear a lot of people say 'javelian' to refer to the sport in which the athlete who throws the spear the farthest wins. Not sure why someone might have inserted that extra 'a'. The right word is 'javelin'.

Javelin, something you wish you could drive right through your Hari Sadu-like boss, who is always breathing down your neck, asking you to 'speeden' up (and not 'speed' up) things, failing which you become the target of some of the 'choiciest' (and not 'choicest') expletives. Come to think of it, you could even unleash your pet 'Pomerian' (and not 'Pomeranian') on your boss.

Finally, this chapter would be incomplete if we do not talk about one Indianism from the travel world. Many a traveller has also made a mess of the word 'itinerary', quite a few going with the much simpler 'itinary', or even saying anything that makes pronouncing this tongue-twister of a word simpler.

It is not that difficult actually. The best way to get our pronunciations right is to actually read the words that we find difficult very carefully, paying close attention to all the vowels and how they are pronounced. Just this simple trick can solve more than half of our enunciative dilemmas.

## 59

# Parts of Indian Cars

The suited and booted salesperson that the car dealership had sent had come prepared for a long haul. A guy buying a fancy car could be a nightmare for the most seasoned of salespersons. There are sure to be so many complex questions about the specifications, features and what not. That is probably why this one started with the easier stuff first.

He explained how the car had one of the best music systems in its class, gave decent average despite being a high-end car, boasted a sunroof and a moonroof to enjoy the view, had a dicky that was large enough to accommodate two fully grown humans, and was equipped with a run-flat stepney should the need ever arise.

That I hardly had any questions must have been a pleasant surprise to him, just like his choice of terms and understanding of concepts was to me. A 'music system', a car that 'gives good average', a 'dicky' and a 'stepney' are words used only in Indian English. As for the 'sunroof' and the 'moonroof', those qualified as techno-linguistic errors.

To begin with, a 'music system' is not even a real word or concept, and native English speakers would hardly ever use such a term to refer to something as specific as a 'car stereo'. And that is pretty much the case with our obsession with a vehicle's 'average' too.

'Average' is simply a statistical concept that refers to the mean or median value. 'Mileage' is a fairly accepted option, although informally. Formally, it refers to the total number of kilometres a vehicle has travelled. That is why advertisements for second-hand cars in the UK highlight the vehicle's 'low mileage', unlike Indian ones that show off the car's 'great mileage'. And vehicles do not 'give' a good 'average'. They are simply 'fuel-efficient' and have a low fuel consumption.

As for the word 'dicky' or 'dickey', it was actually a British colloquial dysphemism for a 'rumble seat', funnily also known as the 'mother-in-law seat', which was an uncovered seat at the rear of the car. Manufacturers eventually covered that part of the car and it came to be used to store luggage. It is known as 'boot' in British English and 'trunk' in American English.

The word 'stepney'—an archaic word that is no longer in use—finds its origin in the Stepney Iron Mongers company. It was the first company to equip cars with an inflated spare wheel and tyre assembly. The more accepted word today is a 'spare tyre' (spelt as 't-i-r-e' in American English).

About the sunroof and the moonroof bit, the thing is that a car cannot have both. A moonroof, by essence, is a panel that is fixed, whereas a sunroof is a glass or opaque panel that slides open to let air or light in.

And by the way, 'dim' or 'upper', and 'dipper' are also part of Indian English. Those are simply 'low (or dipped) beam' and 'high beam' in English. This might come as a surprise but there is also no such thing as what we call a 'brake'. We use the word 'brake' generically to mean something that is used to stop a vehicle. However, the brake assembly is a unit comprising several parts such as the brake pedal, brake drum, etc. So, walking into a store selling spare parts and asking them 'to give you a brake' won't work. You will actually have to name the part, for example:

*'I want a pair of brake levers.'*

What I have always done to get technical terms right is 'Googled' the 'exploded view' of things. Once we know what a part is called, we are only a step away from using the right word for it.

# 60

## Means to an End

You have probably heard of the phrase 'a means to an end'. It refers to a thing that is not valued in itself but is useful in achieving a larger purpose.

That is probably how our relationship with the verb 'to mean' is. The way some of us use this verb is wrong. However, it still does help us in achieving our aim of being understood.

In certain parts of India—depending on the local languages that influence the construction of a sentence in English—you will often hear people make a statement or express an opinion, and then use the verb 'means' to go on to explain what they meant. Here is an example of something I heard recently:

> *'Our teacher is so boring! Means, no one really likes the way she teaches.'*

The urge to use the word 'means' probably comes from how we use words like 'याने (*yanay*)', 'यानी (*yani*)', 'माने (*manay*)' or 'मतलब (*matlab*)', literally Hindi options for 'that is' or 'meaning'; or even 'म्हणजे (*mhanjay*)', literally Marathi for 'meaning'. You will find parallels in most Indian languages.

Obviously, this is not the right way to say it. Informally, I have heard native speakers of English use the word 'meaning' or 'meaning to say' (and not 'means'). Although it is not wrong to use these options, it is best we stick to what is formally more acceptable and grammatically more correct.

'Means' is actually short for 'it means' or 'I mean', or even for 'what I mean to say is that'. So, if that is what is intended, then it's best we use one of these options, isn't it? The above sentence will therefore be better constructed in this manner:

> 'Our teacher is so boring! *I mean*, no one really likes the way she teaches.'

Or,

> 'Our teacher is so boring! *What I mean to say is that* no one really likes the way she teaches.'

And by the way, there is also another way to say this. You can use the Latin 'id est'. Remember the 'i.e.' that we have been using since our school days? Right. That 'i.e.' is an abbreviation for 'id est' that means 'that is (to say)'. It is used when introducing a definition or when explaining a statement that we have made, in order to make it more understandable. It is considered a little more formal in usage, although it is fairly common in informal usage too. Here is an example:

> '*I am a vegetarian, i.e., I do not eat meat, fish or any other animal products.*'

So, pick your options, depending on how colloquial or formal you want to be.

And yes, much like 'i.e.', we also used a lot of 'e.g.' back in school. Well, that comes from 'exempli gratia' and means 'for example'. 'E.g.' is used to introduce examples (and not to introduce definitions or explain statements). For example:

> '*There are some very intellectually challenged politicians in India, e.g.,_____, _____ and_____*'

Well, you know who they are. So, feel free to fill in those blanks.

# 61

# Mornings, Afternoons and Evenings

*'Do you want to watch a movie tomorrow evening?'*

Haven't we all used 'tomorrow morning' or 'tomorrow evening' in a conversation in this manner at some point in time? Of course we have used it, and so have many others around us. So, why do you think I might have asked you this rhetorical question?

Well, as you probably guessed by now, somewhere there lies a trap. Let us take a look at a mistake we make so often and probably never even realise it.

The thing is that although saying 'tomorrow morning' or 'tomorrow evening' is perfectly acceptable, saying 'today morning' or 'today evening' isn't. That is probably inspired by how we say it in our mother tongues; for example:

आज सुबह (*aaj subha;* literally, Hindi for 'today morning')

आज शाम (*aaj sham;* literally, Hindi for 'today evening')

आज सकाळी (*aaj sakaali;* literally, Marathi for 'today morning')

आज संध्याकाळी (*aaj sandhyakaali;* literally, Marathi for 'today evening')

It is no surprise, then, that 'today morning' or 'today evening' doesn't sound wrong to us.

But then, there is also that bit that relates to the idiomatic expression. Although both 'today' and 'tomorrow' are adjectives that can be used to qualify the nouns 'morning' or 'evening', it is not commonly used by native English speakers and might sound odd.

On a subtler note, when referring to times closest to now, native speakers tend to use 'this' more than 'today'. The long and short of it is that we would integrate better with native English speakers if we say 'this morning' or 'this evening', rather than stick out for using 'today morning' and 'today evening'. After all, isn't that why we learn languages? To help us integrate better with speakers of that language?

And just so you know, although saying 'today morning' and 'yesterday night' is wrong, saying 'in the morning today' or 'yesterday, at night' is perfectly correct. Just saying!

# 62

## Past Perfect

I once found myself in an extremely embarrassing situation when, at my friend Aditya's wedding reception, I went up on stage to wish the couple and ended up asking him why Ruchi was not to be seen anywhere. Ruchi was his ex, the girl he had been dating for over a decade and until very recently. I can never forget the disbelief on Aditya's face and the amused look in the bride's eyes.

Aditya is still married, and appears reasonably happy too. I have therefore chosen to believe that my dim-witted question did not cause much damage. But exes can be a tricky topic, especially when your better half has the nose of a hound and the sixth sense of a Sherlock Holmes. It can be equally tricky to choose between the words 'ex' and 'former', terms that look interchangeable to a lot of people.

'Ex'-prime minister and 'former' prime minister, 'ex'-boyfriend and 'former' boyfriend—you will find both words being used fairly often. Is one of them more right than the other? Well, not really. It is just that they mean different things, that's all. Although there has been some debate about whether they are synonyms, the general consensus seems to be that one of many from the past is a 'former', whereas the most recent one is an 'ex'.

So, if a man has been married a few times in the past, each of his previous wives could be referred to as his 'former' wife. However, only the one he divorced last would be called his 'ex'-wife. The same logic will apply to prime ministers, principals, and what have you. That also brings us to two more similar sounding words: 'past' and 'previous'. Again, these are not exactly synonyms.

'Previous' is an adjective that indicates that something existed or occurred before in time, and that it is no longer the case now. If I am the previous owner of an apartment, it means that I no longer own it and that the apartment has a new owner now. 'Previous' also has the sense of 'the one immediately before the current one', for example: your 'previous' job.

'Past' is more generic in nature and refers to anything that belongs to a former time. In a way, it is very similar to 'former'. That is perhaps why you might have heard people use 'former' and 'past' interchangeably when talking about presidents. That is also perhaps why you will hear people say 'immediate past president'. The use of the word 'immediate' gives it the sense of 'ex' (the one before this one) rather than 'former' (one of the many past ones).

Using the right word will always save you from being misunderstood. As for saving yourself from your spouse's fury when formers and exes come back to haunt you, well, you could simply try praying hard, and hope for the best.

# 63

## On Our Own Trip

There are phrases we Indians use so casually and confidently that it never really crosses our mind that we could be speaking or writing incorrectly, or that we could perhaps not be understood well by native English speakers. Sample this as an example.

You are busy guzzling down one chilled beer after another, lying on a hot sunny beach, and your phone rings. It is your customer on the line. He wants an update on his project. Ensuring your voice does not betray how tipsy you are feeling, you tell him that you are 'out of station' and that you will check with your team and call him right back.

This 'out of station' is an example of the kind of phrases I was referring to. Not only is it very archaic, but it is also terribly odd to the native ear. Its usage dates back to the British Raj, when officers used to be posted at 'stations'. If someone called in the officer's absence, they were told that the officer was out of station.

We probably picked this one up from our ancestors, who were likely influenced by their *sahib* (a form of address for a British man in pre-Independence India). But unless you fancy looking like someone who woke up after a hundred years, this phrase is best avoided, unless you are speaking to an Indian.

Fortunately, we have options to pick from. You could go with anything from 'I am travelling' and 'I am away' to simply 'I am not in (*name of your city*)'. Keep it simple, keep it modern!

## 64

## Passing the Parcel

Work takes me to Europe fairly often and eating at restaurants has always been the norm. What has struck me every time I have eaten at a restaurant in Europe is how rare it is to see any leftover food on people's plates. That might probably be because of the portion sizes or perhaps because it is not very common in the West to share food. Each person orders a dish for themselves.

Now, compare that to an Indian family eating at a restaurant. There is sure to be a disproportionate amount of food on the table as compared to the number of diners. We Indians generally order too much food, and our portion sizes are not particularly small either. That is probably why we need to use the word 'parcel' so often.

Firstly, the idea of 'parcelling' leftover food is very Indian. Secondly, 'parcel' is not the right verb to use. This verb is used more in the context of sending or receiving goods by post. As for a 'food parcel', it is a collection of basic food items that are distributed to those in need in times of crisis. So, we should be asking waiters to 'pack' our leftover food, not 'parcel' it.

Sometimes, we also walk to a nearby restaurant or eatery with the intention of getting home something to eat. When you do that the next time, make sure you tell them that you want a 'takeaway' and not a 'parcel'.

Talking about restaurants, here is a fun question. How will you tell someone that there are plenty of restaurants in the city where they could eat, but without using the word 'restaurant'?

Come on, don't rush to read the answer. Give it a moment. Think!

Here is how native speakers would say it:

*'There are plenty of places <u>to eat out</u> in the city.'*

'To eat out' means to have a meal in a restaurant. Beauty often lies in not stating the obvious, and it is always interesting to see how native English speakers do that.

---

### 'Medical Shop'

Repeat a lie often enough and it becomes the truth. 'Medical shop' is a word that is used so rampantly in India that it does not sound wrong, even by a teeny-weeny bit. But that is not the right word. Shops that sell medicinal drugs are called 'pharmacies'.

## 65

## Petrol Problems

South Indian English has its own share of peculiarities, be it the obvious 'h' that makes its presence felt in people's names, turning the 'Sandeeps' and 'Shantis' of the rest of India into 'Sandheeps' and 'Shanthis' down south, or then how the 'h' is pronounced as *haitch* instead of the more regular *aitch* elsewhere in the country.

As odd as such peculiarities might seem, one could at least attempt to defend these with some etymological, grammatical or idiomatic logic. But how can one explain the hundreds of 'petrol bunks' that exist in South Indian English, or how Indians go to 'petrol pumps' to tank up their vehicles?

What is so strange about 'petrol pumps'? Well, unlike what Indians have always believed, a 'petrol pump' is not actually a place. It is a thing! It is that piece of equipment installed at a petrol station to dispense fuel into the fuel tank of a vehicle. So, the place where we go to buy fuel is a 'petrol station' and not a 'petrol pump'.

A petrol station is an establishment that sells petrol and oil. Also known as a 'service station' in the UK, it is called a 'gas station' or a 'filling station' in the US. As for a 'petrol bunk', it is simply India's contribution to the English language, nothing more! And 'fuel' is a generic word. 'Petrol' ('gasoline' in American English) and 'diesel' are types of fuel.

And here is a fun Indianism to end the chapter with. Decades ago, the average Indian home used *rockel* or *ghaaslet* to fire up stoves and lamps. These fuel were so common that hardly a day passed without hearing these names. But turns out we got the pronunciation all wrong. Rockel was actually 'rock oil', a low grade dark oil, and ghaaslet came from 'gas light' referring to the North American Kerosene Gas Light Company that sold lamp oil under the brand name Kerosene.

## 66

## Picture This

If Darwin was indeed right about evolution, then I fear humans will soon have one hand that is longer than the other one. How else would human biology support our hilarious fixation with selfies?

Fingers gripping the phone awkwardly, one hand stretched to its absolute limit, the other displaying a victory sign, gaze fixed high up on the lens, chin pointing forcefully down, face wearing a plastic smile, lips pouted and an apocryphal swag to the entire being—now, if this is not funny, then I do not know what is!

And all this effort just for that perfect click, the one that would go up on our social media profiles as that perfect display picture. Well, to be fair, what photos people upload and how they click it is none of our business. However, we should stop calling it a 'display picture', or the more popular 'DP'. That is neither grammatically right nor colloquially used by native speakers of English.

A display picture is a kind of a tautology. A 'picture' simply means an image and a 'display' means an image that is shown on a screen. A 'display picture' would therefore only mean an image that is shown on a screen; it could be any random image and any random screen.

However, what we mean when we use the term is a picture that represents our social media accounts in all our interactions. And since we use such pictures on our social media profiles, the right word to use would be a 'profile picture'.

And do also make sure you pick the right picture for the right profile. Having a party or a beach photo as your profile picture on professional accounts is nothing short of an Indianism in itself!

# 67

## Tickets and Us

Nothing can really match up to Indian English, especially when it comes to complicating what is otherwise pretty straightforward and simple to say. Take the case of movie tickets, or any other tickets for that matter, and you will see what I mean.

So, your favourite movie releases this Friday and you want to catch a show on the first day, come what may. What do you do? Obviously you buy tickets well in advance to avoid disappointment. Simple, right? But wait, there are some of us who actually 'remove tickets' instead of buying them! And then, there are also some who 'take out tickets'. Quite creative, I must say.

However, it is not very difficult to guess where we get this idea of using verbs such as 'to remove' or 'to take out'. Again, it is because that is how we say it in most Indian languages, isn't it? Look at these examples:

तिकट निकालना (*ticut nikaalnaa*; literally, Hindi for 'to take out or remove tickets')

ਟਿਕਟ ਕੱਢਣੀ (*ticut kadni*; literally, Punjabi for 'to take out or remove tickets')

The निकालना (nikaalnaa) or ਕੱਢਣੀ (kadni) is perhaps the reason why we do not think twice before using the verbs 'to remove' or 'to take out', even though these are not the right verb–noun collocations.

And although 'buy tickets' is indeed the right verb–noun collocation, you can use it only as long as you have actually bought some tickets. Wondering why that is so? Well, that's because there are some tickets that you can 'book' but might not be required to 'buy' immediately. Think airline tickets! If you book through a travel portal or even a travel agency, you will be able to book your ticket and pay for it in a few days.

'Booking tickets' only has the sense of 'reserving tickets'. It does not necessarily mean that you bought them. So, the verb–noun collocation 'buy tickets' and 'book tickets' are not interchangeable, as they mean different things. Using the right verb–noun collocations will do wonders to the quality and impact of your English.

While on the topic, let us also clear any confusion there might be about a host of nouns relating to films that look like synonyms. Most of us will use the nouns 'picture', 'movie', 'film' and 'cinema' interchangeably, and an even larger number of us might be clueless whether a 'theatre', a 'movie theatre', a 'movie hall' and an 'auditorium' mean the same thing.

Let us first brush up on some history and start with the most basic understanding of these terms. Once upon a time there were only 'pictures' (paintings, photographs, etc.). With the advent of technology, these 'pictures' started moving. That was when the term 'motion pictures' (American English) was coined.

'Motion pictures' came to be known as a 'movie' ('film' in British English). Early movies were silent, just as they were colourless. When 'movies' began having characters who you could hear 'talk', they came to be known as 'talkies' (American English). Technically speaking, 'movies' are produced on a thin flexible strip of plastic that is called the 'film'.

Then, a 'cinema' is a place where films are shown (known as a 'movie theatre' or 'the movies' in American English).

However, 'cinema' can also be used as a mass noun to refer to the production of films as an art or industry; for example:

*'The stalwarts of Indian cinema.'*

A 'theatre' is a building or outdoor area where plays are staged. It can also be used to refer to a play, or other activity or presentation considered in terms of its dramatic quality. An 'auditorium' is simply a part of the cinema or even of the theatre where the audience sits.

And unfortunately, a 'movie hall' is not even a word. Fortunately, a 'cinema hall' is, but only in Indian English.

So, if you are in India, you don't need to worry. Pick a noun and a verb of your choice and use it freely. People will understand you no matter what you say. After all, a rose by any other name will still smell just as sweet, at least in our country.

However, if you are in the UK, you better say that you are going to the 'cinema' to watch a 'film', whereas if you happen to be in the US, you would want to say that you are going to the 'movie theatre' to watch a 'movie'.

And yes, it is 'to watch' and not 'to see' a film. If we really get down to the definition, 'seeing' is simply noticing or becoming aware of someone or something, whereas 'watching' is to look at or observe attentively over a period of time.

Sometimes, to get it right, you just have to keep it simple!

## 68

## No Lights

So, let's get this one straight! Lights can 'fade' or lights can even be 'dimmed', and an electric lamp might 'not function properly' anymore, but it isn't really possible for either of them to physically 'go' somewhere, like you know, walk or run away on their own. Wouldn't you agree? In Indian English, however, not only lights (whatever that means; I will come back to that a little later) but even electricity, it seems, can come and go. Such a free world, I must say.

> *'Lights just went a while ago. I will reply to your email as soon as the lights are back.'*
> Or,
> *'Electricity has gone. I will reply to your email as soon as it comes back.'*

These are some of the creative ways of entertaining yourself, if you are living in India. Why do we speak like this when this is not how the native speakers of English would say it?

It could possibly be our *jugaad* (a flexible approach to problem-solving) mentality that encourages us to say pretty much what we want because we know that we will be understood. So, someone somewhere comes up with these peculiar ways of saying things and before we know, everyone is using it.

Then there is also the influence of our mother tongues. In

most Indian languages it is perfectly normal to say something like:

लाइट आ गयी / चली गयी *(light aa gayi/chali gayi)*; literally, Hindi for 'lights came/went')

ਵੱਤੀ ਚਲੀ ਗਈ / ਆ ਗਈ (*vatti chali gayi/aa gayi*; literally, Punjabi for 'electricity went/came')

ಕರೆಂಟ್ ಬಂತು /ಹೋಯಿತು (*current bantu/hoytu;* literally, Kannada for 'current came/went')

No wonder, then, that lights and electricity are treated like moveable objects when we speak English.

And mind it, you cannot even say you 'have' or 'do not have' lights or electricity. Of course, you do have both of them. The electric circuit was invented in 1827 and the electric bulb was invented in 1879.

So, what is the correct way to say this? Well, when 'electricity goes' or when 'lights have not yet come back', you can simply say that there has been a 'power outage'. Use this the next time your local electricity board fails you.

And don't worry if people don't understand you, or if the use of such technical words is met with baffled or bemused looks from your interlocutors. Take the time to explain to them what this means, because this is one Indianism that we need to get rid of if we want to be understood better globally.

And yes, here is a little something about the 'lights' part, as promised. Using words such as लाइट (light), इलेक्ट्रिसिटी (electricity) or करेंट (current) might work in Hindi or in most Indian languages, but please be mindful of the fact that to a native English speaker, the word 'lights' (plural form) does not in any way mean 'electricity'. It simply means 'decorative illuminations'. Even the word 'light' (singular form) primarily means a source of illumination, especially an electric lamp. So do not use 'light', 'current' and 'electricity' interchangeably. They mean very different things.

> ### 'On One Hand'
>
> This sounds familiar, right? But familiarity is also a breeding ground for mistakes. Did you know that the right way to say it would be with the definite article 'the'? It is always 'on the one hand', just like it is always 'on the other hand', and not 'on other hand'.

# 69

## Ruled by the Ruler

Teachers of yore took great pleasure in making liberal use of that big fat wooden ruler. I know it because my reluctant knuckles and scarcely cushioned bums have been uneasy recipients of dozens of those blows throughout my school life. The stoic look of satisfaction on the teachers' faces as their ruler chased my withdrawing knuckles and dodging bums, was a sight many of my classmates noticeably enjoyed.

Like most people, we too grew up believing that this weapon of choice was called a 'ruler'. And then one day, I heard someone call it a 'scale'. And thereafter, I have seen people use these two words interchangeably many times. So, here is what you need to know on the topic.

A 'scale' can actually be any device that has a series of marks at regular intervals and can be used for measuring something. In that sense, a ruler is a scale, but every scale need not be a ruler. Think thermometer! It has a scale too, but we do not call it a ruler. A 'ruler' (also called a 'rule') is a strip of wood or other rigid material used for measuring length or marking a straight line.

Then, there is also the 'rubber' or 'eraser' conundrum. Simply put, erasers are made of rubber, just as they can be made of vinyl too. So, technically speaking, the better word to use would be an 'eraser', but that is American English. The British call it a 'rubber'. But don't you ask an American for a rubber. Funnily, in the US that is slang for a condom.

What is equally funny is that Indians have long believed in the existence of the 'compass box'. That is actually the name of a whisky company, not a box used to store pens and pencils. Those are stored in a 'pencil case' or a 'pencil box'. As for a compass, it is only one of the few instruments in a geometry set that comes in a tin box.

English grammar and vocabulary can indeed be a bottomless pit. The more I read and research, the more it dawns on me how we are never too far from an Indianism.

# 70

## Perfecting Our Pronunciations

I have always had just this one way of spelling my name: Sandeep Nulkar. And I have always been called 'संदीप नूलकर' no matter which part of India I am in. However, the moment I step out of India, people call me 'सॅनडीप नलकार'. Initially, I used to wonder what was so difficult about my name. It is not like my name was Uvuvwevwevwe Onyetenyevwe Ugwemuhwem Osas (world's hardest name, it seems).

It was only much later that it dawned on me that the reason probably was the skewed ideas of pronunciation that our ancestors believed in. That is perhaps what has ensured that we Indians got the English spellings of our names so wrong that we made it extremely easy for foreigners to mispronounce them.

Here is what we are taught: 'A' says 'अॅ', 'E' says 'ॲ', 'I' says 'इ', 'O' says 'ऑ' and 'U' says 'अ'. Now, against the backdrop of this information, if you look at how ancestral influence has made me spell my name, you will see why foreigners have a tough time getting my name right. Since 'A' says 'अॅ' and 'U' says 'अ', they pronounce 'san' as 'सॅन', 'deep' as 'डीप', 'nul' as 'नल' and 'kar' as 'कार'.

So, how do I ensure they get it right? Well, to begin with, I will need to make peace with the fact that some of them will continue to say 'डीप' and not 'दीप', since many foreign languages are not likely to have the sound 'द'. And then, I need to start spelling my name as 'Sundeep Noolkur'. That should ensure they get it almost right, barring the 'डीप' that is.

So, have you been spelling your name correctly? How would you spell it now that you have read this chapter? It is probably too late or even quite unnecessary for us to change the way we spell our names now, but we might surely want to consider using a phonetically more apt one wherever possible.

And puh-lease do not pronounce 'message' as 'मॅसेज', 'parents' as 'पॅरेन्ट्स' and birthday as 'बड्डे'. It is मेसेज, पेरेन्ट्स and बर्थडे.

# 71

## Pressure Cooker

Indian cities are like giant pressure cookers, bursting at their seams with far too many people and way too little space. The cacophony of overcrowded places, congested streets, cramped offices and matchbox-sized homes provide the perfect backdrop for the unending problems of urban life. These factors make words like 'tension', 'stress' and 'pressure' a part of our day-to-day vocabulary.

Indian English makes these words seem like synonyms to us. But that is not as problematic as when we think that tension, stress or pressure can be 'given' or 'taken' and make 'taking' it look like a matter of choice. Many of us have been guilty of advising a loved one to not 'take' tension or then perhaps committed the felony of complaining about how someone or something is 'giving' us tension.

Well, to begin with, tension or stress cannot be 'given' or 'taken', nor are these contagious. So, it is not quite possible to 'get' tension or stress either. People 'are' tensed or stressed. They can even be 'under' considerable stress. While trying to soothe someone, native English speakers would probably just say something as simple as 'relax', or use 'stress' as a verb and say 'do not stress'.

And by the way, these are not synonyms either. Although 'tension' and 'stress' do nearly mean the same thing, the word 'pressure'—except in Indian English—is not used to refer to mental or emotional strain. Rather, it points to the influence or effect of something, or to the use of persuasion to make someone do something.

That is probably why some of us need to smoke a cigarette first thing in the morning. It persuades our body to build the 'pressure' needed to poop. This seems to be a purely Indian trait too. So, take a chill pill instead and do not stress over this pressure thing, and who knows, it might just happen without a fag.

# 72

## Pretty Cars

Travelling in a Mumbai taxi at night is an experience like no other. As you cruise along Marine Drive, drunk on the buzz of the city that never sleeps, the cool night breeze hits your face while you stare into the infinite darkness of the mighty Arabian Sea. Altaf Raja croons in the background, leaving you to reminisce about the love stories that could never be.

The blue lighting in the taxi sets the mood as the funky upholstery draws you in. Tassels dangle from the rear-view mirror and right beneath it is the mini sanctum, with god figurines and flowers decorating its surroundings. The showpieces and the mini fan on the dashboard grab your attention, while the furry steering wheel cover, a flashy gear-lever crest and the crocheted curtains complete the all-too-familiar look.

Be it the Mumbai taxi or a private car, Indians can seldom do without (over)doing up the interior. Believe it or not, this practice itself is a kind of an Indianism. You would rarely come across a car decked up from the inside in most countries, while ours will invariably look like a virtual house on wheels. No wonder then that we have 'car decor shops' at every nook and corner.

But did you know that 'car decor shops' exist only in India? In the English-speaking world, they merely have stores that sell car spares and accessories, and not so surprisingly, such stores have names like 'ABC Car Spares' or 'ABC Car

Accessories'. They are not called 'car decor shops' like they are in India.

And since they do not think of themselves as 'car decor shops', none of them offer a range of decorative items as elaborate as that in India. Some stores do offer a car interior-modification service though, but those are more of structural and design changes, and not decorative ones.

Finally, what you do with the interior of your car is your prerogative, but please make sure you gift yourself a taxi ride at night the next time you are in Mumbai.

---

### 'Parallely'

Although they did tell us in school that we can form an adverb by adding '-ly' at the end of an adjective, doing that to 'parallel' is wrong. There is no such word as 'parallely'. It is always 'in parallel'.

# 73

## Shifting Out

I remember the verb 'shift' being used frequently in school. We often asked friends to shift so that more of us could squeeze ourselves onto a bench. Sometimes, parents scolded us when we shifted from English to our mother tongue and back to English while speaking. Then, doctors shift patients to the ICU if their condition worsens. And by now, we know enough people who shift into their dream homes or to better cities. Clearly, Indians have enriched the verb 'shift' with meanings that native speakers would find hard to comprehend.

When we want someone to make some place for us to sit, the right verbs to use would be 'scoot' or 'move' and not 'shift'. Similarly, when we change to a different language while speaking, we are technically 'switching' between languages and not 'shifting' between them. Doctors, too, should be 'moving' patients to the ICU, and not 'shifting' them there. As for new houses and different cities, we do not quite 'shift' into them. We 'move' to a new city or even 'relocate' to one, much like we move into a new house.

I hope all this rhetoric isn't making the verb 'shift' seem taboo, because it is not. It is a legitimate verb that means to move something from one place to another, especially over a small distance. You could use it in a sentence in this manner:

*'The service personnel shifted the electric cables away from our house.'*

It is wrong to use the verb 'shift' when referring to animate objects. When used to refer to inanimate objects, 'shift' is generally used more in a temporal sense. For example:

*'I shifted my class from Monday to Wednesday.'*

Moving into a new house reminds me of 'flats' and 'apartments'—words that have very different connotations for a native English speaker. In India, people buy a 'flat' that is located in an 'apartment'. An apartment, to us, is a multi-storeyed building that has several flats on every floor.

However, to the native speakers, a flat cannot possibly be located in an apartment because the two mean the same. To the British, a 'flat' is a suite of rooms whereas an 'apartment' is still a flat but an upscale one. What the British call a flat, Americans call an apartment.

So, whether you are moving into a new flat or an upscale apartment, you will most certainly need to 'Google' for 'packers and movers', because you are never really going to find 'packers and shifters', are you?

## 74

# Please Don't Kill Anyone

We were such innocent souls when we were in school. We believed in miracles and that God could make those happen for us. We petitioned to Him for better grades, pleaded with Him to save us from the wrath of our parents whenever they were summoned by our teachers, and begged Him every time we needed the universe to conspire to make it all right for us.

And then, we grew up and became smarter and richer. We still continued to believe in miracles and in the fact that God could make those happen for us. However, we stopped bargaining with Him. Instead, we started making deals with Him, using food or hard cash as mediums of exchange. But what did not change was the fact that He remained as important.

And this importance assumes especially epic proportions in India, where anything important is called God (think Sachin Tendulkar). It seems pretty logical then that 'God promise' is a legitimate concept in Indian English. After all, fellow Indians find it easier to trust us if we invoke God when we make promises, as everyone knows that we can neither afford to piss Him off, nor dare invite His fury by lying under oath.

Unsurprisingly, nearly every Indian language has a word for 'God promise'. Take a look at these examples:

भगवान की कसम (*bhagwaan ki kasam*; literally, Hindi for 'God promise')

देवाची शपथ (*devaachi shapath;* literally, Marathi for 'God promise')

ભગવાનના સમ (*bhagwaan naa sum;* literally, Gujarati for 'God promise')

ਰੱਬ ਦੀ ਸੌਂਹ (*rub di saunha;* literally, Punjabi for 'God promise')

ದೇವರ ಆಣೆ (*devar anay;* literally, Kannada for 'God promise')

This was probably why we invented the concept of 'God promise', which, by the way, is not understood beyond our borders.

It is the same with our love for our mothers. Nearly every Indian language also has a word for 'mother promise', which incidentally is at par with 'God promise'. But then, what good are we if we do not add that special Indian touch to something? So, we created 'mother-die promise'. A term particularly popular among children, it reassures the listener that we aren't lying and that we are even willing to bet our mother's life in an effort to make the listener believe us.

The idea of putting the life or the existence of something dear to us on the line in an attempt to assure people that we are not lying is very Indian. When native English speakers want to affirm that something is the case or want to promise to do something, they simply swear on a person or thing dear to them, or even to God, but not on their life. And they certainly do not use terms like 'God promise' or 'mother-die promise'.

I cannot even begin to speculate how these Indianisms would be understood or received beyond India. Let us just reserve Indianisms for Indians! So, keep your gods in your thoughts and your mothers in your hearts, and don't promise them away.

## 75

# Rest in Peace

The purpose of bringing this up is not to shame anyone, so I am not going to name this Hindi movie that I was watching a while ago in which the very filmy protagonist was shown writing a letter to his family. A voiceover was narrating the contents of the letter and, as seems to be the trend nowadays, English subtitles were attempting to make the life of the non-Hindi-speaking audience easier. I say 'attempting' for two reasons. Firstly, most subtitles have this uncanny knack of making serious movies look hilarious, and secondly, the subtitles for this movie were particularly cringeworthy. At some point, the protagonist says:

'बाकी सब ठीक है' (*baaki sub theek hai*; literally, Hindi for 'remaining everything else is fine')

The subtitles for this part read:

*'Rest all is ok.'*

Come to think of it, this isn't very surprising. This wasn't the first time I was hearing it. I mean, we live in India! How far can we be from an Indianism! 'Rest everything is fine?', 'rest OK?' or 'all else OK?' are common questions that you can expect to hear colloquially. Why just questions, a certain review on a popular travel platform even says, 'Bad service... Rest all OK...'

No points for guessing where the inspiration is coming from. It is indeed from our mother tongues. Here are some examples:

बाकी सब ठीक है (*Baaki sub theek hai*; literally, Hindi for 'rest everything is fine')

বাকি সব ঠিক আছে (*Baaki soab theek achay*; literally, Bengali for 'rest everything is fine')

બાકી બધું બરાબર છે (*Baaki baddu baraabar chay*; literally, Gujarati for 'rest everything is fine')

बाकी सगळें बरें आसा (*Baaki saglay barein aasaa*; literally, Konkani for 'rest everything is fine')

While we know that this literally translates into 'rest everything is fine', none of it should be translated literally into English. This is not how it is said or even something that would be clearly understood. The right way to ask this in English is:

*'How is everything?'*

And the right answer would be:

*'Everything is fine.'*

I know that this does not satisfy our urge to use the word 'else'. But I guess we are going to have to do without it when conversing with non-Indians. It's not like native English speakers would never say it, but it is not very common.

And by the way, the word 'OK' (also 'okay') is informal, although it is used rampantly even in formal conversations these days. 'OK' is written in capital letters and can be used as an exclamation, an adjective, an adverb, a noun and even a verb. It is written in capital letters probably because it is short for 'Old Kinderhook', the nickname for former American President Martin Van Buren, who popularised the slogan 'orl korrect' during his re-election campaign.

# 76
# Sit and Do What?

This really needs to be said once and for all! See, we can sit and thereby be 'sitting'. We can also do something while we are sitting, like read a book or sing, or whatever else you fancy. However, there are some things we simply cannot do, like 'sit for' or 'sit to' do something.

Initially, I thought this was just about a few people. However, over a period of time, I have heard this one Indianism from numerous people cutting across states and regions. And then, recently, a friend of mine was over for lunch. He chatted for a bit and then he asked me:

'Can we <u>sit for</u> lunch? I am really hungry.'

Obviously, this is wrong. But wait till you hear the worst I have heard. I have actually heard someone say:

'Let's <u>sit for food</u>?'

As you might have guessed, this is indeed the influence of our mother tongues, showing up in the way we construct English sentences. Here are some examples:

खाना खाने बैठें (*khaana khanay baithay;* literally, Hindi for 'let's sit to eat food')

भोजन करने बैठें (*bhojun karnay baithay;* literally, Hindi for 'let's sit to do a meal')

ಉಟಕ್ಕೆ ಕೂತುಕೊಳ್ಳಿ *(Utakke cout kolli;* literally, Kannada for 'sit for food')

जेवपाक बसुया *(Jevpaak basuya;* literally, Konkani for 'let's sit for a meal')

I am sure there are other Indian languages, too, where one uses the verbs 'sit' and 'eat' together and that is what possibly causes these mistakes.

However, we do not need to complicate things. What works here are some really simple and grammatically correct options such as:

*'Let's eat! I am hungry.'*

Or,

*'Can we eat, please? I am hungry.'*

That being said, there is another similar sounding but grammatically correct phrasal verb that you can use. It is 'to sit down to a meal' (not the same as 'to sit for lunch' or 'to sit for food'). 'To sit down to a meal' means to sit and eat together.

And then, there are 'sit-down meals' too. A 'sit-down meal' is simply a meal eaten sitting at a table. It allows you to choose menu options per course ahead of time. This is how you can use these:

*'We were tired from all the walking. But later in the afternoon, we could finally <u>sit down to eat</u> a delicious meal.'*

Or,

*'I prefer <u>sit-down meals</u> to buffets.'*

Like you can see here, phrasal verbs and prepositions can often be the difference between the right and the wrong way of saying things.

> ### 'Parlour'
>
> When a woman tells you that she is going to a 'parlour', people in India know exactly where she is going. However, the use of the word 'parlour' in isolation can create some amount of confusion for native English speakers. To them, a 'parlour' is traditionally a sitting room in a private house or even a room in a private building to receive guests. It would help if we did not eat up words and called it a 'beauty parlour'.

# 77
## Sex

Some people might be tempted to look over their shoulders while reading this chapter, at least until the title is still in plain sight. Sex can be such a taboo topic in our country. So, you can imagine how that could make pulling someone's leg so much more fun, especially when stories involving the frowned-upon-word are spun.

That is exactly what happened with this nerdy kind of a guy back in college. I am not sure whether there was any truth to the tale but some of his not-so-nerdy friends took immense sadistic pleasure in narrating how this chap wrote 'occasionally' in the column titled 'sex' when filling out a certain form. The poor guy had to listen to this story every time someone mentioned the word 'form'.

Speaking of forms, we are required to fill in one ever so often. And although the information we are asked to provide might vary, what usually makes it to every form is the section sometimes titled 'sex' and sometimes 'gender'. But these seemingly interchangeable words are actually not so.

To begin with, the use of the word 'sex' is grammatically and politically incorrect in the context of a form. In fact, there is even a government guideline in the UK that suggests that unless the context is medical the use of the word 'sex' should be avoided, even when asking a person their gender. The recommended word is, in fact, 'gender'.

And since our dear Americans love going against anything

resembling the norm, they find nothing wrong in using the word 'sex'. In fact, some of them go a step further and accuse the Brits of being prudes who shy away from using the 'S'-word because they find it too hot to handle. Grammatically and medically speaking though, I would side with the Brits.

'Sex' refers more to the biological and physiological characteristics of a person. 'Gender', on the other hand, refers to cultural and social differences and can include a broader range of identities. It is therefore possible to be of a gender that is different from one's sex.

At a time when society is finally becoming more accepting of the LGBTQIA+ community, understanding the difference between these words and using them correctly has become even more important.

# 78

## Repeat Offenders

Have you ever been asked to 'repeat' something 'again' or to 'combine' something 'together', or heard someone talk about their 'future plans', been promised a 'free gift', or at least been asked to withdraw some money from an 'ATM machine'?

Do you see what I see? 'Repeat' includes the meaning of the word 'again', 'combine' includes the meaning of 'together', we can only 'plan' for 'future', a 'gift' is always 'free', and the 'M' in 'ATM' stands for 'machine'.

Welcome to the world of redundancies. And it is not something that just other people do. Each one of us has probably been guilty of using a few redundancies every now and then. So, what are redundancies, why do people use them and what is wrong about using them?

Well, redundancies are basically the use of two or more words that convey the same meaning. No one really knows why people use redundancies, but it would be safe to say that these are used inadvertently, for the most part. And although people might hardly notice the redundancies in our speech, a text infested with redundancies is sure to have a negative impact on the reader or listener.

So, even if you feel like something is incomplete or amiss, do control the urge to use such words. It is perfectly adequate to say the following:

*'Please <u>repeat</u> what you said.'*
*'Please <u>combine</u> the two.'*
*'If you buy this product, you will get a <u>gift</u>.'*
*'Please withdraw money from the <u>ATM</u>.'*

The Internet can give you dozens of examples of the many redundancies that plague our language. Simply go through any comprehensive list and you will quickly spot the ones you are guilty of using. Thereafter, it is only a matter of remembering to not use those.

# 79
## 'Sixteen Going on Seventeen'

I know some men (usually bosses) who will grow a beard only to look a little older to their subordinates. I also know some women who, for the life of them, do not want to look as old as they actually are. Age is such a sensitive topic that, one way or another, nearly everyone seems to be faking it.

Ask a woman her age and she will probably just smile it off with:

*'You never ask a lady her age!'*

Do that with a man and it gets a little more complicated. The ones who know they look much younger will wear a broad grin and instantly quiz you saying:

*'Let's see if you can guess.'*

And the ones who have resigned to fate and accepted their big paunches and barren heads will suddenly get very factual. They will either tell you how old they exactly are, right down to the number of weeks, and perhaps even days, or then use this classic Indianism and say something like:

*'I just completed 50, now <u>running</u> 51.'*

Remember the famous song 'Sixteen Going on Seventeen' from the iconic movie *The Sound of Music*? Right, that is how you say your age in English, if you are hell bent on being very specific. But you really do not need to be any more specific than this. Speaking generically, just giving a simple number as an answer should be more than enough.

In English, you 'are' a certain age ('*I am 20 years old*') before you 'turn' a year older ('*I will turn 21 this year*'). And when you are between two ages, you are simply 'going on a certain age' ('*I am going on 21*'), which means you are approaching a specified age. Make sure you do not use any other verb, barring these ones, when talking about your age.

## 80

## So Fresh

Somewhere in India, a husband who has just returned from nowhere important has just coaxed his wife into making some tea for him while he goes and 'gets fresh'. Elsewhere in India, a prick of a man is also 'getting fresh', but with someone else's sister, catcalling a popular Bollywood number that is suggestive of the things he would like to do with her should she respond to his overtures.

Two distinct situations, and yet, in both these cases our protagonist seems to be doing the exact same thing—'getting fresh'. Something doesn't seem right, don't you think?

Tired Indians come back home and love to 'get fresh' before they get on with things. 'Fresh *honaa*', no matter what language you speak, is a thing in India. Older Bollywood movies always showed the dutiful wife or the loving mother asking the man to get fresh while they made him some tea. However, that would simply be 'freshen up' to native English speakers. To 'get fresh' actually means to be uncivil towards someone, especially in a sexual way.

This talk about 'fresh' also reminds me of yet another Indianism that is so deep-rooted in our day-to-day language that we would struggle to believe it is not grammatically correct. I am talking about the new entrants in colleges, who are referred to as 'freshers' in India. Why, we even have 'freshers parties' for them.

Well, just so you know, these are totally Indian inventions. Native speakers call them 'freshmen' and 'freshwomen', and although this does reek of patriarchy, both freshmen and freshwomen go to 'freshman's parties'. My apologies, but there are no 'freshwoman parties'.

On a parting note, let me tell you what I saw on one of my trips down south. A highway restaurant had actually called their toilet a 'fresh room'. You can't beat that!

---

### 'Purse'

A large part of North India feels that 'purse' means 'wallet'. Sorry to break hearts here, but all that it actually means is a leather or plastic pouch used to carry money, and that too, typically by a woman. Even to Americans, a purse would mean 'handbag' and not 'wallet'.

# 81

## Such a Comprehensive Bath

Indians seem to be making path-breaking contributions to the art of bathing! Throughout history there have been references to various types (therapeutic, public) and kinds (dry, sponge) of baths. However, there has been nothing in recorded history that beats the specificity of the kind of bathing modern Indians seem to be indulging in.

I am referring to the favourite Indian ritual of 'head baths', something that leads to a mother somewhere nagging her daughter about having a head bath now that it is the weekend finally, or some woman in a hostel telling her friends that she will take a little longer in the bathroom today because she plans to have a head bath.

Although a 'head bath' could be something that is very well understood in our country, I am not too sure it will mean much to anyone in the English-speaking world. And funnily, what we mean to say does not even have anything to do with our 'head'. It is more about our 'hair'. Case in point being that there are no head baths in English. Native speakers simply 'wash their hair', or 'shampoo and condition' it.

Shampoo reminds me of how a lot of Indian languages have contributed words to the English language. Shampoo is one such word and Hindi is one such language. 'Shampoo' comes from *chāmpo* (चाँपो), the imperative form of the Hindi verb *chāpnaa* (चाँपना) that means 'to press'. For example, *sir chāpna* (सिर चाँपना) means 'to massage the scalp'.

I think I know how I am going to spend my Sunday this week. I will wake up late, go to the neighbourhood hair-cutting saloon ('a barber shop' in native English), get myself a nice *chumpi* (head massage), and then come back and shampoo, condition and wash my hair. Sounds like a plan, eh?

# 82

# Small Small, Different Different

I am sure we have all heard at least one hardworking housewife complain about how she is practically left with no time for herself because 'small small' things take up so much of her time in the kitchen, or perhaps we've met that employee who was so happy with the lavish spread at the conference because they got to taste 'different different' things.

Does something seem wrong to you in these sentences? Haha! The question itself is rhetorical. Why would I even ask you such a question if everything was hunky-dory?

Using adjectives twice and not even realising it, or worse still, thinking that it is indeed the correct way to use them, is the influence of Indian languages.

We Indians spare very few adjectives. So, be it the 'big big eyes' or the 'red red roses', we are never far from hearing these grammatical blunders that would only make a native English speaker smile from ear to ear.

बड़े बड़े शहरों में ऐसी छोटी छोटी बातें होती रहती हैं।

*(Baday baday shehron mein aisi choti choti batein hoti rehti hain.)*

Literally, Hindi for: *'Such small small things keep happening in big big cities.'*

Remember this famous line from the Hindi film *Dilwale Dulhania Le Jayenge*? This, you can say, is the crux of why we Indians love repeating adjectives.

You will see this habit of repeating adjectives in most Indian languages, for example:

ছোটো ছোটো (*choto choto*; literally, Bengali for 'small small')

বেশি বেশি (*beshi beshi*; literally, Bengali for 'more more')

व्हडलें व्हडलें (*vhadlay vhadlay*; literally, Konkani for 'big big')

If we are used to hearing or saying something like this, then blurting out English sentences with adjectives appearing twice isn't going to seem very difficult to us, I guess. But in English, this is not the norm.

Why do we Indians use adjectives twice? Well, we do that for emphasis. When we say, 'small small', we mean 'really' small, like we mean 'really' different when we say 'different different'. We also use them twice because it is grammatically correct to use such structures in most Indian languages.

But then, what do native English speakers do when they want to emphasise something? They do not even enjoy the luxury of repeating adjectives! Well, they simply don't use them twice, or they use adverbs. For example:

'It is the small things in life that give the most happiness.'

Or,

'They have these shirts in a lot of different colours.'

The point I am making here is quite simple. When we speak English, we must make sure we are not firing the same adjective twice, one after the other. Let us give people one less reason to be confused or amused!

# 83

## Staying Abroad

Ever noticed how some people love to show off their children who have lived or studied abroad, and how some others give factual and minimal information if their children have only lived or studied within India?

I call it the colonial hangover. It makes anything associated with a developed, first-world country appear to be way cooler. And if we find it cool, then we also want to shout it from our rooftops and let the world know. So, we did the unthinkable. We actually coined an amazing word for it. I will tell you what that word is a little later in the chapter.

Let me first tell you about another word with which you can use only a specific preposition. I am talking about 'abroad' and the fact that 'from' is the only preposition that can be used with it. Now, you might wonder why I am telling you this. Well, that is because some people think it is all right to say things like:

*'My father is going to abroad next week.'*

Or,

*'He does not live here. He lives in abroad.'*

We can trace the origin of our urge to use such prepositions back to our mother tongues. Here are some examples:

वह विलायत में रहता है *(waha vilaayut mein rehtaa hai;* literally, Hindi for 'he lives in abroad')

तो गावाला जाणार आहे *(toh gaawaalaa jaanaar ahay;* literally, Marathi for 'he will go to a city')

Let me tell you why these sentences are wrong. You see, prepositions can only be used with nouns or pronouns. That is what happens when you say sentences such as:

*'All passengers returning from abroad need to be screened for the virus.'*

You are using 'abroad' as a noun and hence you can use a preposition with it, and 'from' is the only grammatically-correct one to use.

However, it is not the correct usage when you say something like:

*'My father is going <u>to abroad</u> next week.'*

Or,

*'He does not live here. He lives <u>in abroad</u>.'*

You are using 'abroad' as an adverb and it is not correct to use prepositions with adverbs. The other reason why you cannot use the prepositions 'in' or 'to' with 'abroad' is because the word already has the sense of 'to' and 'in', as it means 'in or to a foreign country'.

And since we used the verb 'live' in the above examples, let me also tell you that 'to live' and 'to stay' aren't exactly synonyms. 'To live' is used to indicate permanent residence, whereas 'to stay' is used to indicate a place where someone stays temporarily. For example:

'I *live* in Beverley Hills.'

But,

'I like to *stay* at the Taj whenever I travel to Goa.'

And now, back to that amazing term that we Indians coined. The word is 'foreign-returned'. Firstly, it is not a word that would even be understood beyond India. Secondly, there is certainly no glamour that Westerners would attach to it even if you were to explain what it means.

Having lived or studied in a foreign country would sound about as glamourous to Westerners as doing that in any Indian city would sound to some Indian parents. It is best to avoid using this home-grown adjective completely, in India or elsewhere. Neither would we make any point, nor an impression.

# 84

# Tring! Tring!

How we Indians love to talk! Whether it is with that poor fellow sitting beside us on a train journey or with our near and dear ones over an unending phone call, we hardly need a reason to start a conversation. But then, like all good things, even our phone calls have to come to an end. And that is when we utter this pearl of an Indianism:

*'Ok, bye! I am getting late. I will keep the phone.'*

You see, in the days when mobile phones did not exist, you could actually put down the handset back on its cradle. So, it made sense to use the verb 'to put down'. However, today, when most of us use mobile phones, we only tap a button to end a call. At the most, we put the phone away (in our pockets or purses), but we don't really 'put down' the phone to end a call anymore.

However, since we did put down phones back then, most Indian languages found a way to say exactly that. Here are some examples:

फ़ोन रखना (*phone rakhnaa*; literally, Hindi for 'to keep the phone')

ફોન રાખવું (*phone rakhvu*; literally, Gujarati for 'to keep the phone')

Not many of us will therefore find the above sentence to be wrong. There is also no chance we would ever be misunderstood if we were to use it in India. But wrong it surely is. Say 'I will keep the phone' to a native speaker of English and perhaps the first thing that will come to their mind is not 'OK, bye' but a very surprised 'where' or 'why'.

They would probably be left wondering as to where exactly you intend to keep the phone or why you are keeping it somewhere at all. And who knows, it might even bring a smile to their face—the kind that lights up ours, when we see a foreigner trying hard to impress us with an awkwardly pronounced 'Naa...maa...stay'.

To recap, in English you do not say 'I will keep the phone' unless you *actually* want to say that you want to keep the phone (the telephone instrument) somewhere (on the table, in its regular place, etc.). 'To keep' simply means to put or store in a regular place. What you can simply say is:

*'Ok, bye! I am getting late. I will hang up.'*

Some native speakers also use 'to put the phone down on someone' (in the sense of 'to hang up on someone'), or 'to put down the phone' (in the sense of 'to hang up'), but those have a slightly archaic origin, since we do not 'put down' (or 'hang up') phones anymore.

One last thing about phones! If you ask someone who is holding the phone to their ear but not talking, whether the other person is on the line, a likely reply you might get in India is:

*'Yeah, but they have kept the phone on hold.'*

The thing is, you cannot 'keep the phone on hold'. The one you are 'putting' (and not 'keeping') on hold is the person, and not the phone. So, the right way to say the above sentence would be:

*'Yeah, but they have put me on hold.'*

And, by the way, it is also incorrect to tell someone to 'please hold'. That might funnily give rise to the questions 'why' or 'how'. What one should be doing instead is asking people to 'please hold the line'. Now, that would ensure you don't cross any grammatical lines.

> ### 'Rawal Plug'
>
> This is what many Indians believe to be the right pronunciation for that wooden or plastic twig-like thing that carpenters insert in the hole in your wall before they drill the screw in. The actual word is 'Rawlplug', pronounced like 'crawl' without the 'c' plus 'plug'. Rawlplug is a brand that sells wall plugs. So, unless we are using wall plugs of the Rawlplug brand, we should just simply call them 'wall plugs'.

## 85

## Sunny Side Up

Kids hardly need a reason to tease their friends. Short or tall, thin or fat, cool or dorky, they will still find a way to pillory you, like my friends did. They used to call me *mhataryaa* (oldie). Reason? I had a diastema (sorry, just showing off—I mean a gap) between my upper incisors.

And then of course, we also had those unfortunate few who were called *dhapnyaa* or *chusmiss* (both are slangs for those wearing specs), or even *dolus* (sarcastic way of referring to someone who despite being able to see acted like someone who can't). Trust kids to make something as normal as wearing specs look like a grave misfortune!

Speaking of 'specs', it is just one of the many names we use to refer to our eyewear. Spoilt for choice, I have seen many people use the wrong one as much as I have seen them use one to make a style statement. So, here is a quick lowdown on what's what, starting with the two broad categories: 'spectacles' and 'sunglasses'.

The stuff that the chusmiss-es of the world wear are called 'spectacles', and they are used to correct our vision. 'Spectacles' is a word that is always used in the plural unless you call it 'a pair of spectacles', which is its singular. Colloquially, they are called 'specs' or '(eye)glasses' (because lenses used to be made of glass earlier).

'Sunglasses', the ones that film stars bafflingly wear at night unlike us, are simply meant to protect our eyes from the sun's

UV rays. People also call them 'goggles', 'shades' or even 'glares', depending on how stylish they want to appear. Not all of these words are synonyms though.

'Goggles' are slightly different from sunglasses, since they have side shields. 'Shades' are the same as sunglasses but it is a word that can only be used informally. As for 'glares', it is simply someone's imagination running wild. It does not even come close to meaning sunglasses.

That settles the what's what debate then. Coming back to our favourite film stars sporting sunglasses, a little bird once told me that they wear them at night to hide the puffy eyes they get from lack of sleep. Here's wishing them a happy *ninny*. Chashm-e-Baddoor!

# 86

## The Action Continues

If you have not watched the British sitcom *Mind Your Language*, then I can assure you that you have not watched much! It was hilarious for more reasons than one—the characters, the accents and above all, some genuinely authentic comedy arising out of the grammatical errors and cultural differences among the students of English from all over the world.

What struck me the most in nearly every episode, however, was the overuse of the present continuous tense by the Indian and Pakistani characters. Humour, they say, always has an element of underlying truth, and truth be told, Indians seem to have a liking for this tense, especially when it comes to the verb 'to have'.

Statements like 'I am having 30 years of experience' or 'he is having fever' (it is 'a fever', by the way) are some of the many in the present continuous that you will hear around you all the time. Obviously, that is not right and ergo, the need for this chapter.

The thing is that the verb 'to have' can be used both as a stative (one that shows a state of being) and a dynamic (one that shows temporary action) verb, and it is grammatically incorrect to use stative verbs in the present continuous. That is why 'I am having experience' or 'I am having fever' is wrong, but 'she is having a baby' or 'we are having friends over' is not.

So, when is it right to use the present continuous tense then? Well, here are seven situations in which you could use this tense without any hesitation.

The present continuous can be used to talk about something that is happening at the moment of speaking, for example:

*'The baby is playing in the garden.'*

Or to talk about something that is temporary (but is not a state of being); for example:

*'I am having a bath.'*

Or then to talk about something that happens recurrently; for example:

*'She is always smiling.'*

You can also use the present continuous to talk about something that is changing; for example:

*'Your English is improving.'*

Or to talk about something that happens at a certain time; for example:

*'At 6.00 p.m. I am usually driving back from office.'*

Or then to talk about something that is new; for example:

*'These days most people are watching movies on their mobile phones.'*

Surprisingly, we can also use the present continuous to talk about the future, for example:

*'I am taking a course in Arabic next summer.'*

Now, take a quick break and go watch an episode of *Mind Your Language*. The present continuous will hit home harder, I am sure.

# 87

## Sweet Tooth

Cadbury captured the absolute essence of Indian celebrations with their '*kuch meetha ho jaye* (how about we eat something sweet)' tagline. Western festivities can be all about the roast turkeys, the stuffed chickens, or even the herbed butter snails with only a small, almost pretentious, sweet towards the end. However, our festivities are always excessively about something sweet. Blame it on our insatiable sweet tooth!

That is perhaps why every Indian family will have tales of how some forefather could down copious amounts of their favourite sweetmeat. That *nanaji* who could eat a jaw-dropping kilo of *laddoo*s, or that *chachaji* who could polish off two dozen drool-worthy *roshogolla*s, or then someone from the younger generation trying to live up to the pedigree by consuming a dozen steaming, *ghee*-dripping *modak*s.

No matter what our chosen poison is, it is all fine until we are relishing it during a meal. However, the moment we switch to a Western style of eating and decide to end a meal with something sweet, for some strange reason we choose to call it a 'sweet dish'. That is strange because the English language has no such word. Native English speakers simply call it a 'dessert', which is a sweet course eaten at the end of a meal.

And if you are confused between 'desert' and 'dessert' like I used to be, here is a trick I used in order to remember which one is which. 'Dessert' spelt with a double 's' is for the sweet stuff ('ss' for 'sweet stuff'), whereas 'desert', spelt with a single 's', signifies the barren land where there is too much 's'-and and hardly any water.

# 88

# Take It or Leave It

*'Oh! So, you are Mr Sharma's classmate's cousin!'*

The typical Indian will not rest until they have figured out how you are connected to someone or something that they are connected to as well. That makes asking a lot of questions mandatory. We need to know where people are from, where they have studied, what they do for a living, who their friends are, what their family members do and so much more.

There is also something else Indians cannot do without, and that is doling out unsolicited advice. Whether it is about how *Kailas Jeevan* or *kapaalbhaati* are the best remedies for practically every ailment ever, or what we think someone should be doing with their life—we are always a step away from crossing the line.

Be it out of our need to know how we are connected to the other person, or then out of our instinctive urge to give people our two cents' worth on every topic, we do end up being nosy for the most part. So, some people, in an effort to not come across as that, will start an intrusive question with a 'please don't take it otherwise'.

Unfortunately, this is only a typical Indianism that has no place in the English language. Moreover, apart from being grammatically incorrect, this can even come across as a threat that has been left incomplete. You know like:

*'Please don't take it otherwise...or I will beat the s\*\*t out of you.'*

Jokes apart, here are some simple options you could go with, depending on what you would like to ask or advise:

*'If you don't mind me asking, are you married?'*
*'Do you have children, if I may ask?'*
*'I hope you don't mind me saying, but this soup needs some more salt.'*

And no matter what option we pick when being at our inquisitive best, it will still always be wrong to ask someone their age or salary.

---

### 'Saloon'

It is seemingly a place where Indian men go to get their hair, or whatever is left of it, chopped. In native English, however, it can mean anything from a public building used for a specific purpose to a lounge bar where alcoholic drinks are served (American). We can simply call it a 'barber's shop' (or a 'barbershop' if we are in the US).

# 89

## Take Your Pick

You know that phrase people use in formal letters that are addressed to no one in particular? Yes, that one—'to whom it may concern'. I find it to be a peculiarly funny phrase. It sounds as if we are writing a letter to someone but have no clue to whom. It must be weird for the recipients too. It might just give them the impression that they are reading a letter meant for someone else.

That is exactly how I feel every time I read a letter or an email that starts with 'greetings of the day'. What on earth does that even mean? It almost sounds like the sender wanted to wish me but did not know what exactly to say and is, therefore, asking me to pick a greeting that I like from the tons of greetings there are.

Greeting people this way is a typically Indian thing to do. Nonetheless, on some level, it also looks like a pretty smart idea. It saves us the trouble of deciding whether or not to address the person by their name, and helps us avoid calling them 'Sir' or 'Ma'am', 'Mr' or 'Ms', especially when we are not sure who will end up reading our email. It also allows us to not commit by wishing someone a 'good morning' when they could very easily be reading our letter or email in the evening.

Native English speakers do not play any such games. They simply use a 'good morning', 'good afternoon', 'good day' or what have you. The closest they will come to being this generic is when they say something like 'season's greetings'. You will see that being used mostly around festive seasons, although it might still come across as cold and unfriendly.

As for the phrase that I used as an analogy in the first paragraph, the right way to say it is indeed 'to whom it may concern' and not 'to whomsoever it may concern', as is commonly used in India. It is a legitimate way to start a letter, notice or testimonial when the identity of the recipient is unknown.

## 90

# We Are Like That Only

The heading of this chapter reminds me of this friend of mine from England, who was travelling through Rajasthan some years ago. And as is the norm with most Westerners who visit this incredible state, she had hired a local tour guide who spoke English. Towards the end of her trip, intrigued by how happy Indians seemed to be in general, she asked her guide as to how we managed to smile through all the poverty and hardships. Beaming with pride, the guide replied:

*'We are like that only, Madam!'*

'We are like that only' is probably one of the most telling examples of an Indianism. It seems to be so popular that not only Indians but even native speakers of English have used it to point out the difference between 'us' and 'them'. From being used as the name of a book on understanding the logic of the Indian consumer to being the title of articles in British and American media, 'we are like that only' has come to depict how we are as people as much as it reflects how we speak English.

But what is wrong with this sentence? Well, it has the word 'only' that has been used in a way only Indians do. Native speakers will never say that. They would perhaps say something like:

*'That's just how we are.'*

We use 'only' to satisfy this strong urge we have to use a word for emphasis. Like much else, the source of this urge can be traced back to our mother tongues. Here are some examples:

ही (*hee*; literally, Hindi for 'just', 'precisely', 'merely')
कल ही कहा था मैंने (*kal hee kahaa thaa mainay*; literally, Hindi for 'yesterday only I told you')

ਹੀ (*hee*; literally, Punjabi for 'just', 'precisely', 'merely')
ਕਲ ਹੀ ਤਾਂ ਕਿਹਾ ਸੀ ਮੈਂ (*kal hee taa kihaa si mai*; literally, Punjabi for 'yesterday only I said')

च (*cha*; literally, Marathi for 'just', 'precisely', 'merely')
मीच सांगितलं तुला (*meech sangitla toola*; literally, Marathi for 'I only told you')

च (*cha*; literally, Konkani for 'just', 'precisely', 'merely')
हांवेंच सांगिल्लें तुका (*haavench sangillay tooka*; literally, Konkani for 'I only told you')

Saying 'yesterday I told you' or 'I am like that' or 'I told you' will simply not give us Indians the same satisfaction as when we say:

*'Yesterday only I told you.'*
*'I am like that only.'*
*'I only told you.'*

When we use 'only', we get the feeling that we have conveyed the intensity and intricacies of our sentiments. But this is not how you say it in grammatically correct English. The first two sentences ('Yesterday only I told you' and 'I am like that only') are better constructed in the following manner:

*'I just told you yesterday.'*
*'That is just how I am.'*

That way, you will get all the emphasis you need, but not end up using the word 'only' incorrectly.

As for the third sentence ('I only told you'), it is an excellent example of how it can mean different things to different people. In Indian English, 'I only told you' means that I (and no one else) was the one who told you something. However, to native English speakers, this same sentence means that the thing was told only to them and to no one else. This practically means opposite things as you can see.

We must therefore not use 'only' for emphasis or in the sense of 'just', and especially not at the end of sentences or after subject pronouns. Native speakers will not get the emphasis we are trying to lay by using such a word. They will simply misunderstand us or find it funny.

# 91

## Very Costly Indeed

There are some words in the English language that have the potential of surprising us Indians. All we need to do is look them up in a dictionary and our beliefs will lay shattered. I am talking about words that we have known to mean something all our lives but this cruel dictionary will tell us that they mean something else entirely. Life nearly seems like a lie!

One such word is 'pricey'. To most Indians that would mean a person who is playing hard to get, or a person who is never available. We all have that one friend who never has time to spend with us, and is therefore chided with a sentence like this:

*'Why do you always act so pricey?'*

Now, here's what you could do. Open up any dictionary, an online one if you will, and look up what 'pricey' means. Simply put, it is an informal word for expensive. That's it! Most words would have dozens of meanings but this one doesn't even have two. It's just this one meaning. Of course, you can always trust us Indians to enrich such poor words with additional meanings and, in this case, we did exactly that.

I think the word 'pricey' was coined owing to the influence of an informal phrase used in a few Indian languages. This phrase contains a word that means 'price'. People use the phrase 'भाव खाना (*bhaav khaana*; literally, Hindi for "eat price")' or 'भाव

खाणे (*bhaav khaanay*; literally, Marathi for "eat price")' when they want to suggest that a person is deliberately adopting an aloof or uninterested attitude, or is rarely available. Such phrases are there in most Indian languages.

However, these examples should clear any confusion there might be:

> '*Her <u>pricey clothes</u> still did not make her look classy.*'
> '*What does she think of herself? Always <u>playing hard to get</u>!*'

The important point to note here is that although we Indians use 'to act pricey' in any context, 'playing hard to get' is usually used only in the context of dating.

## 92

## What Sound Was That?

The sweet sounds of 'OK, *lah*', 'No, *lah*' or 'I'll see you tomorrow, *lah*' have melted many a heart that has set foot on Singaporean soil. The locals can be heard using these sweet nothings at the end of most sentences, often leaving tourists baffled. Try as much as they do, tourists find it difficult to understand why the locals produce this sound ever so often.

Cut to India, and we produce our own versions of this sound. To complicate matters, it's different for every Indian language. Those are a lot of sounds for the foreign ear!

From the social butterflies of the Lutyens to the 'chatterati' of South Mumbai, and everywhere in-between, the affluent Indian's English is infested with the 'ना (*naa*)'. From the prodding 'come, *naa*' and the remorseful 'but you never want to study, *naa*' to the pleading 'let's go home, *naa*' we use question tags as freely as we possibly can.

But what are question tags and why do we use them? Well, a question tag (in British English) or a tag question (in American English) is a very short clause at the end of a statement that changes it into a question. And we use them precisely for this reason—to convert a statement into a question.

I know what you are thinking. And yes, you are right. Question tags do have an Indian-language connection and that is precisely why they are being covered in this section. So, what's the connection we are talking about? To understand it better, let's look at these sentences:

आओ ना (*Aa o naa; literally,* Hindi for 'Come, naa')

लेकिन तुम तो कभी पढ़ना ही नहीं चाहते ना! (*Lekin tum toh kabhi padhnaa hi nahi chahtay naa; literally,* Hindi for 'But you never want to study, naa')

घर चलते हैं ना! (*Ghar chaltay hai naa; literally,* Hindi for 'Let's go home, naa')

When someone uses a 'naa' in such sentences, what they are doing is unknowingly creating question tags. But aren't question tags legitimate? Why then is it a problem if people use them? Well, the problem arises when people say the entire sentence in English but leave the question tag 'naa' as it is in Hindi. And when we do that, we too end up producing a sound that foreigners will not understand.

But what do we mean to say when we use a 'naa'? Here is what we actually mean to say in English:

*'Come, <u>will you</u>?'*
*'But you never want to study, <u>do you</u>?'*
*'Let's go home, <u>shall we</u>?'*

Here are some types and examples of question tags for you to build a better understanding of the subject:

*'He'll be here by noon, yeah?'* (Universal tag)
*'So, you aren't coming tonight, right?'* (Universal tag)
*'I am done with him, I am.'* (Statement tag)
*'He was a good singer, he was.'* (Statement tag)
*'Turn the volume down, will you?'* (Imperative tag)
*'Let's eat, shall we?'* (Imperative tag)

Question tags aren't peculiar only to Hindi. Konkani-speaking people use a lot of 'न्ही (*nhi*)', 'मरे (*maray*)' or 'मगो (*mago*)'.

Gujaratis can also be found using the 'ને (*nay*)' and Bengalis use a lot of 'না (*naa*)' too. I have also heard a lot of 'ಡ (*da*)' in Bangalore.

So, here is what I suggest we do. When speaking in English with foreigners, let us avoid using question tags from our mother tongues. When speaking in English, use English question tags!

However, if we are feeling a little adventurous or want to fit in, we can consider using question tags from the local language, even when speaking in English. After all, ending some sentences with a 'lah' while in Singapore can surely make us look like less of a tourist.

---

### 'Scholar'

The nation needs to know once and for all that a 'scholar' is not a synonym for 'intelligent' or 'clever'. Originally, 'scholar' meant 'student'. Eventually, it also acquired the meaning of someone who held a scholarship or someone who is a specialist in the field of humanities.

## Testing Times

School life used to be swarmed with all kinds of tests and exams. Barely a few days would pass before another one was imminent. For most of us, this felt like a fairly unnecessary exercise in our otherwise happy life. With little desire to burn the midnight oil, most students simply took the road less travelled.

From peeping into forbidden papers and 'mugging up' the 'most likely' questions to dolling up our papers in the hope that we would somehow scrape through, we did it all. And yet, I came close to being called 'Sir Isaac Newton', a name my friends used to sarcastically tease the pea-brained classmates who earned single-digit marks.

For what those tests and exams were worth, they surely created some truly testing times for most of us. They still do for some people, I guess, especially when they are torn between what word to pick—a 'test' or an 'exam'. Are these synonyms and can they be used interchangeably?

Well, the thing is that a 'test' need not even be related to academics. It can be related to any field. However, an 'exam' (short for 'examination' and also referred to as 'exams') is mostly an academic or medical exercise. An exam is also more formal, more important and more elaborate as compared to a test, and is conducted for a broader range of topics.

And yes, before we move on, let us bust some more myths. 'Mugging' means attacking or robbing someone, something that scoundrels do, and is certainly not how students prepare for exams. And no, you cannot even use 'by hearting' as a verb, although you can say 'learning by heart', 'learning by rote' or even 'memorising'.

## 94

# The Both-Handed Writer

From my personal experience of having learnt a few foreign and some Indian languages, I can tell you how there are times when one simply does not remember the right word or phrase to convey something. And therein lies the beauty of the English we speak—a language we hijacked from right under the watchful eyes of the people who call it their own.

When speaking in languages that are foreign to us, we all pause, fumble or even struggle to find the right word sometimes. However, when we speak English, no such predicament befalls us. The audaciously confident lot that we are, we effortlessly avoid the word we do not know by replacing it with a group of words that mean the same thing.

This is something that dawned on me when, the other day, I heard someone proclaim with immense pride how their son was able to write and do much else with 'both his hands'. Now, to a native English speaker that would have simply meant having a son who was 'ambidextrous'.

So, while there is nothing wrong in flaunting our English or saving the day with a group of words, sometimes it is worth our while to learn all the right words.

After all, as much as a certain Mr Tharoor might be the butt of some linguistic trolling, don't we all love it when he speaks the kind of English that only he can, and shows the natives how it is done?

## 95

# Thank You

One day, at some station on the London Underground, I found myself standing behind an Indian gentleman at the ticket counter. When it was his turn, the gentleman quickly announced where he wanted to go. But instead of acting on his request, the lady at the counter simply wished him 'good morning'. A little confused, the gentleman repeated his request, only to be wished 'good morning' yet again. This happened a couple more times before the lady realised that her sarcasm was not working. Finally, she asked him point-blank if he would mind wishing her a good morning before blurting out his request.

Every language represents a culture that has a set of rules of social etiquette. One cannot, therefore, speak a language and forget to respect these rules. However, a lot of us are guilty of just that when we speak in English. I am sure we have all ordered coffee at our favourite café and not wished the barista who took our order.

Native speakers of English will rarely be found making such rookie mistakes. They will always greet people appropriately, depending on the time of the day and on how formal or informal the occasion is.

Speaking of manners and thank yous, there is another Indianism that needs to be called out. It is the 'mention not' or the 'no mention' that you will hear some people say when someone thanks them. Obviously, that is not the right thing to say. From the slightly more formal 'my pleasure' and 'you are welcome' to the more informal 'no problem', 'no worries' and 'not at all', or even the friendly 'anytime', there are nearly a dozen options you can pick from. Just make sure you do not forget to say something.

## 96

# The Art of Gifting

Depending on the kind of parents we are, a child turning a year older can be a big deal. Birthday celebrations can be more a reflection of our values and principles than of our love for our prodigal children. From not celebrating birthdays at all to having themed and destination ones that are hosted by professional emcees, one will get to see an entire gamut of creative ideas at work.

The level of extravagance notwithstanding, our creativity will also be tested when trying to decide what to gift the bunch of kids who show up. After all, our gifts cannot merely be a patch on the lovely presents that they will bring. So, from the more thoughtful indoor plants and DIY kits to expensive toys, the 'return gifts' we give will be a testimony to how high our creative minds can soar.

And our creative minds must have soared high indeed, for someone to come up with the term 'return gift'—an extremely logical term, I must say, and yet very wrong linguistically. Just because it is a gift that we give someone in return does not make it a 'return gift'. Interestingly, native speakers of English call it a 'party favour'. Unlike the Indian return gifts, party favours are not only about birthdays. They are gifts given to guests at any party.

And yes, a 'gift' and 'present' might be synonyms, viewed from a grammatical perspective, but there is a difference in the way they are used. A 'gift' is something more generic that can be given to anyone, and it need not always be a physical item. A 'present', however, is a physical item that is wrapped and presented to people you know well.

Armed with this gift of clarity, you can now start thinking about what presents you would like to buy your loved ones for an upcoming occasion.

### 'Take Rest'

Although most Indians would never suspect it, this popular phrase is not entirely complete because there is an indefinite article missing here. 'Rest' is a noun and nouns are rarely used without articles, definite or indefinite. It is always 'take a rest', much like it is always 'take a break'.

# 97

## The Great Indian Bobble and Other Gestures

You might remember Philippe from an earlier chapter. Yes, that French exchange student who stayed with me. Well, he was the first one to make me realise how hilarious the great Indian bobble could look. To watch Philippe tease us by dramatically bobbling his head every now and then was always a funny sight.

Easily the most remarkable of gestural Indianisms, the head bobble (or wiggle or wobble) is our habit of shaking our head from side to side. It is such an integral part of our body language that we would not even notice it until we catch a foreigner bobble their head. As confusing as it might initially seem to anyone who is not an Indian, they soon decode the plethora of meanings the gesture harbours. Then, there is no greater joy than employing the bobble to convey an array of thoughts.

There are a variety of bobbles: the politically correct, prolonged, slow bobble to assure your whining spouse that you agree with them; or the intermittent, brief and fast bobbles that are the perfect choice to give your boss the impression that they always make so much sense; or the trusted, brief and lazy bobble that could mean a simple 'yes' or even a reluctant 'sure, why not' to ward off that nagging friend; or finally, this same brief and lazy bobble, but now accompanied by raised eyebrows and a smirk, that could mean anything from 'do you think I am stupid enough to say yes?' and 'you are such a smart ass, aren't you?' to 'yes, because I cannot say no'.

And much like the bobble, there are a few more gestures that are peculiar to Indians. My favourites are the quick raising of the chin and eyebrows that replaces the need to say a 'hey', 'hi' or 'hello', and the raised little finger of your dominant hand that points to the urgent need to answer nature's call. By the way, it is this same little finger that we use when we start counting numbers, unlike Europeans who begin counting with their thumbs.

Gestures are crucial when it comes to effective communication. It is important to use them adequately, after ensuring that the ones we use do not happen to be hilarious or offensive in the other culture. Pretty much why one should never cross the index and middle fingers in Vietnam. Far from wishing someone luck (which is what it means in India), it would look like we are giving them the middle finger by gesturing a woman's genitalia.

## 98

# What's in a Name?

Names are just that, names. There will always be those names that you like, and then there will be those that you don't quite like. However, you really cannot have 'good names' and 'bad names', unless of course you are in India, where we seem to have good names, although surprisingly, we do not have bad ones.

Oblivious of the fact that it is wrong, an alarming number of Indians still continue to ask amused native speakers of English, or even Indians who know better, questions like:

*'What is your good name?'*

But why might have we started using the term 'good name'? Well, the way I see it, there is a background to this that is deep-rooted in our culture.

You see, people have started unearthing fancy names for their children only recently. However, that was not the case earlier, when a majority of our names were simply the names of gods. The names of gods, in a God-fearing country such as ours, could not have been anything but शुभ (*shubh*; literally, Hindi for 'auspicious', 'lucky' or 'good'). That is perhaps how the term शुभ नाम (shubh *naam*; literally, Hindi for 'good name') came to be.

'Good name' is a direct translation of शुभ नाम (shubh naam) or the various other parallels we will find in other Indian languages. It is a typically Indian thing to say that simply does not have a parallel in Western culture. Reason enough, then, to drop the 'good' and go simply with name, when speaking with foreigners.

And just so you know, 'having a good name' does indeed mean something in English. It means 'a person's good reputation'. You can use it in a sentence like this:

> *'James Anderson was accused of ball tampering. That ruined the <u>good name</u> he had earned playing the game.'*

# 99

## When Will We Reach?

Picture this! You are taking a road trip to the lovely countryside or to the nearest beach perhaps. Your car looks too small to contain the many people that have managed to crawl inside it. But that's not all. You also have luggage—on the carrier, behind the seats and in every other conceivable gap. And then, there are the children who are restless about when their ordeal (the journey) will end.

Cars could come in different sizes and families could be smaller or the pieces of luggage fewer, but if there is a kid on board, the one thing that will be common across cars in India is the nagging question, 'Mumma! When will we reach?'

The impatient parents will simply reply with a curt 'just shut up for a while', the cunning ones will probably use the new-age trick of silencing the inquisitive child by slapping a mobile phone onto their welcoming palms, while the really patient ones will actually humour their children by telling them when they are going to reach.

There are no right answers to this question, but the use of a couple of words is surely wrong. The first one probably has its roots in the Indian way of asking it. Here are some examples:

हम कब पहुचेंगे *(hum kab pohochengay;* literally, Hindi for 'when will we reach')
ਅਸੀਂ ਕਦੋਂ ਪਹੁੰਚਾਂਗੇ *(asi kado pohuchangay;* literally, Punjabi for 'when will we reach')

You can surely 'reach' things, like you can reach the door before you open it. However, native speakers of English do not use 'reach' when they want to ask when they will reach a certain place. The classic expression that native English-speaking children use to whine from the backseats of their cars is:

*'Are we there yet, Mummy?'*

Or,

*'Will we arrive soon, Mummy?'*

A lot of English-speaking Indian children have started calling their mothers 'mumma'. However, that is not how it is pronounced (with a lingering emphasis on the 'mm') or even spelt.

Even the closest correct spelling, 'mamma', is still quite old-fashioned. It progresses from teeny babies calling their mothers 'mama' and small children calling their mothers 'mummy' to slightly older children or young adults calling their mothers 'mum'. 'Ma' too is quite common in some parts of the UK.

And with that, we have 'reached' the end of this chapter!

# 100

## Who Came and Where?

Earlier in this book, we looked at how there are only a few things we can 'catch', like we can catch a cold, or we can catch a movie or we can even catch our breath. However, what we cannot catch is a place.

The verb 'come' is a bit like that. We can come home to our loved ones or someone can come in a swanky car. Then T-shirts can come in different colours or sizes and as a phrasal verb; for example:

*'The batsman came in at number three.'*

But that's about all that humans can come 'to' or 'in'.

Wondering what the point of this chapter is? Well, it is about the incorrect use of the verb–preposition collocations 'come-in' and 'come-on'. I am sure you have heard people say things like:

*'His name has <u>come in</u> today's newspaper.'*
*'He <u>came on</u> the news this morning.'*
*'You <u>came in</u> my dream last night.'*

The bitter reality is that we cannot come either 'in' a newspaper or 'on' the news, and although coming 'in' someone's dream is possible, wait till I tell you what that could mean to a native speaker. Let me first tell you where the usage of the verb 'come' is coming from.

This is clearly the influence of our mother tongues. Here are some examples:

कौन है जो सपनों में आया (*kaun hai jo sapno may aayaa;* literally, Hindi for 'who is it that came in my dreams')

તે મારા સપનામાં આવ્યો (*tay maaraa sapnaa maa aavyo;* literally, Gujarati for 'you came in my dream')

But if this is wrong, how should we say it then? Well, you can simply say:

'His name was <u>mentioned/featured</u> in today's newspaper.'
'He <u>was in</u> the news this morning.'
'I <u>dreamt of</u> you last night.'
'You were <u>in my dream</u> last night.'
'You <u>appeared</u> in my dream.'

And now, coming to the uncomfortable part. If you say 'you came in my dream' to a native speaker of English, what they will probably understand (or at least think even if they are sure you don't mean to say something as silly as this) is that in your dream they actually had an orgasm.

I can't stress enough how important prepositions are, no matter what you want, whether it is to make an impression or to simply steer clear of an uncomfortable situation.

---

### 'Touring Jobs'

This is what a lot of people call jobs that involve a lot of travelling. However, since 'touring' is not even a grammatically correct word, what they should simply be saying instead is that 'their jobs require them to travel often'.

# 101

## The Silent Admirer

Ravi never ceased to amaze me. His love story with the mirrored walls of our gym could even put some self-obsessed teenagers to shame. It was almost like he put himself through the ordeal of weight training just so that he could endlessly admire every muscle in his body between sets. And he was not the only character around. Gyms can be such entertaining places!

What can also be amusingly entertaining is how the fitness industry attempts to repackage old wine in a new bottle. That is why our good old gym started getting fancier names as the market grew hotter and the competition tougher. First it was the 'fitness centre', then the 'health club', and then the mother of all names, the 'wellness centre'.

I mean, they can call their venture anything they like as long as they do not make us end up in a similar-looking place, because these words have different meanings. They are certainly not synonyms.

To bust the biggest myth, a 'gym' (short for 'gymnasium') was originally not even a place for lifting weights or running on treadmills. It was only a covered area meant for athletics. The word eventually came to be used as slang for a 'fitness centre', which is what we actually mean when we say 'gym'.

A 'fitness centre' is where you go when you lust after those washboard abs. It is a place that provides a range of facilities to help you improve and maintain your physical fitness and health. A 'health club' goes a step further and offers health and beauty treatments, apart from the usual exercise facilities. As for a 'wellness centre', it is pure marketing genius.

Be that as it may, the next time you step into your gym, no matter what it is called, do take a moment to silently admire those who cannot stop admiring themselves. You will surely be entertained!

## 102

# The Number Game

We quickly need to create a list of words that are best left out when we speak in English to non-Indians. And I highly recommend putting the words 'lakh' and 'crore' right on top of this list.

When foreigners hear these words, they will either go blank or feel the need to convert, much like we do when someone gives us a dollar or Euro price. Making them go through this effort makes no sense considering that the purpose of language is seamless communication.

How do we make the communication seamless then? We can start by replacing a 'lakh' with a 'hundred thousand' and a 'crore' with '10 million'. This should work in most cases, but if we really want to ace this topic, then we need a slightly higher level of awareness.

A 'lakh' in India is a 'hundred thousand' in most parts of the world. So, 9 lakh, for example, will be 900,000. Things change a bit from 10 lakh onwards. Ten lakh is a million and 10 million is what we call a 'crore'. It can get a tad confusing hereafter, which is why I am going to use this nice little table.

| In India | Internationally |
|---|---|
| 1 lakh | 100,000 |
| 10 lakh | 1 million |
| 1 crore | 10 million |
| 10 crore | 100 million |
| 100 crore | 1 billion |
| 1,000 crore | 10 billion |
| 10,000 crore | 100 billion |
| 1,00,000 crore | 1 trillion |

Then there is also a 'quadrillion' and a 'quintillion'. However, knowing our sh*t up to a trillion should see us through most situations, unless you are a mathematician or figure on the list of the world's richest people.

## 103

# The Opposite Need Not Always Be True

We all have that one friend whose brain is a virtual Google Maps. There is hardly a road in town they wouldn't know, and that is absolutely great if they are driving. Saves you the co-driving! However, if you are driving and they happen to be sitting beside you, then you bloody well be prepared for one nightmare of a ride.

These enlightened souls take great pleasure in guiding you with smug pride on how to avoid every traffic signal, although you crave to window shop at nearly each one. They will tell you what roads to circumvent in order to avoid the rush, although you have made no such plea. They will not think twice before chiding you for taking a route that they are so damn sure was a 'long cut'.

'Long cut' looks like the perfect antonym of the noun 'shortcut' but is unfortunately not even a legitimate word. Just because 'shortcut' is a grammatically correct word does not mean that its seeming opposite would be too. Native English speakers would simply say that they took the 'longer route' to somewhere, or that they would 'take longer to reach' their destination, since they took the wrong (or longer) route.

There is one more word, by the way, that falls right into the opposite-need-not-always-be-true category, and that is the noun 'prepone'. I am sure you have 'preponed' something yourself or witnessed someone do it. Maybe it was simply a meeting that your boss 'preponed' to suit his fancy, or perhaps an engagement that was 'preponed' by parents who wanted to get it done and over with before anyone changed their mind.

'Prepone' is actually such an apt verb. However, as logical as it might sound, it is a verb that has been 'made in India'. What that means is that if we were to use it internationally, we would risk not being understood clearly and also stand out for all the wrong reasons. In British English, meetings, engagements or events are simply 'brought forward', not 'preponed'.

Native speakers also use the verb 'reschedule', but in a more generic way, to suggest moving something to an earlier or later date or time. Here are a couple of examples to demonstrate the nuances of these verbs:

> 'Our meeting was <u>brought forward</u> to 11.00 a.m.' (it means that the meeting was originally scheduled for later)
> 'Our meeting was <u>rescheduled to</u> 11.00 a.m.' (it means that the meeting could have been originally scheduled for earlier or later)

Whether or not the opposite is true, we absolutely don't need to be apologetic about the words we have invented. After all, they work well in India. Let's just make sure we use the right ones when we step out though.

# 104

## Whistle *Podu*

In every mainstream Bollywood movie, the nation's then prevailing heartthrob has continued to mouth cheesy pickup lines, chant aptly-worded songs and whistle away to glory, all while ignoring the reprimands of the defenceless heroine. This is how we have unknowingly inspired an entire generation of eve-teasers.

As soon as they see anything that even remotely resembles a woman, some desperate men will make their move. That is perhaps why '*toomhaari maa beyhanay nahi hai kyaa* (don't you have a mother or any sisters)' has been the favourite defence of many women against the most persistent of eve-teasers.

But as much as such behaviour needs to be condemned, that is not the subject of this chapter. The word 'eve-teasing' is. A euphemism that can be found only in Indian English, it will not be understood beyond our country, and in a couple of neighbouring countries at the most. The right word for 'eve-teasing' is actually 'public sexual harassment' or 'sexual assault'.

Yes, these are words that convey the actual gravity of what we do to our women. 'Eve-teasing' just makes it sound like harmless fun. There is a fine line between flirting and sexual harassment. Let's just make sure we never cross it, linguistically or otherwise.

# Word to Word and Same to Same

An old friend is in town and wants you to go watch a film with him. He is the same friend who was once caught 'cheating' (and not 'copying', like we call it) in school when the teacher realised that his answer sheet was a 'word to word' copy of yours. Later, as you walk out of the cinema, you ask him how he liked the film and he says it was nice but that he thought it was a 'same to same' copy of some Hollywood film.

Even if this story seems a little contrived to you, I am sure you would agree that you have heard or even used words such as 'same to same' or 'word to word' in various situations. However, they could not be more detached from reality.

It would be hard to imagine why someone might have even come up with a term like 'same to same', when extremely simple options such as 'identical', 'exactly the same' or even 'a carbon copy' have always existed. Apartments on different floors can be 'identical', two things can be made of 'exactly the same' material, or children can be 'carbon copies' of their parents.

Similarly, inventing the adjective 'word to word' was totally unnecessary when grammatically correct options such as 'word for word' or even 'verbatim' were available. Students, for example, can copy down the poems they are being taught 'word for word', and newspapers can give a 'verbatim' account of what a certain starlet said.

However, do not confuse 'word for word' with 'word by word'. The former is about being 'identical' whereas the latter can simply mean 'detailed'. For example, a teacher can give her students a 'word by word' explanation of a poem, or a newsreader can give the viewers a 'word by word' analysis of someone's speech.

Sometimes, it is only a small difference between what we say and what the grammatically correct thing to say is, but that, mind it, makes a world of difference!

---

### 'Vessels'

These are supposedly the pots, pans and dishes that cruel mothers-in-law expect their helpless daughters-in-law to wash. However, vessels are merely 'hollow containers' or perhaps even 'ships' or 'large boats'. The right word to be used is 'cookware'.

# Whose Son Is He Anyway?

It is not very uncommon for people in India to say something like:

> आप ही का बेटा है *(aap hi kaa betaa hai;* literally, Hindi for 'he is your son only')

When a parent says that to someone, what they are trying to tell the other person is that the person means a lot to them and has as much right over the child as them.

That reminds me of a joke that used to do the rounds when I was in school. It was a joke about this Indian mother and her son, living in Canada. One day, it seems, the mother and son were walking down a street near their house, when they met a Canadian couple, who used to be their neighbour long ago. The couple was very pleased to see them after a long time. Unaware that the Indian lady had a son, the gentleman asked her if the charming boy was her son. In response, the Indian lady said:

> 'Yes, John. But obviously, he is your son too!'

I am sure this will never happen in real life. All said and done, this was only a joke. But it surely does remind us of how some of the mistakes we make when we speak English are not always influenced by our mother tongues but by our culture.

As much as one can say something like this in Hindi, one should not really attempt this in English, owing to how culturally different people are in the English-speaking world.

For them, their child is their child, and your child is yours.

Does that mean the Western world does not share our emotion? That they are so dry that they will not feel for someone else's child? Certainly not! It's just that the way they express it (and not necessarily say it out loud) is different, and is also in keeping with their culture.

The most formal and perhaps even religious way the natives accord that honour (right) to someone is by asking them to be their child's godparent. A godparent is someone who the child's parents choose to take care of the child's upbringing and personal development, or even claim legal guardianship for, if anything were to happen to them. Godparents would be the godmother and the godfather, and godchildren would be the godson and the goddaughter.

Informally, though, people in the English-speaking world (Western culture) will not say the exact equivalent of 'आप ही का बेटा है (aap hi kaa betaa hai)'. That is because they have a different understanding of individuality and personal space compared to us. We can say that to someone just to make them feel close to us, but I do not see Westerners doing that.

So, the question is, how do Westerners say this informally? Well, the following sentences are fairly common:

*'He is like a son/daughter to me.'*

Or,

*'He is the son/daughter I never had.'*

It would not be a bad idea to filter content from a cultural perspective, every time we speak in English, and especially with Westerners. Not only will that ensure we aren't misunderstood, it will also not get us into embarrassing situations.

# 107

# Ya-Ya Land

For the longest time, I used to wonder what the 'ya' that a lot of English-speaking Indians use at the end of the sentence was for. At a party if you prod your friend to sing a song, she will shy away saying:

*'Please don't pester me to sing, ya! I really suck at it.'*

I don't know if you have noticed a pattern but 'ए no, ya!' (ए pronounced like the letter 'A') is something I hear a lot from those who have studied in English-medium schools across some states in India. Whether it is the 'please don't pester me to sing, ya' or then the 'ए no, ya', the point is that a lot of people end certain sentences with 'ya'. What is this 'ya', where does it come from, and why do we feel this innate urge to end certain sentences with it?

Before I answer that, let me tell you what this 'ya' is certainly not. It is surely not a shortening of the word 'yeah'. In English, 'yeah' does not have a shortening, and is itself the non-standard spelling of the word 'yes'.

'Ya' is also not a shortening of the word 'you', although the non-standard spelling of the word 'you' is indeed 'ya'. Did you understand why I am saying it cannot be a shortening of the word 'you'? If you didn't, read this sentence:

*'Please don't pester me, you.'*

After I replaced 'ya' with 'you' in this sentence, you suddenly realise that it makes no sense. So clearly, the 'ya' cannot be a shortening of 'you'.

This is getting more and more mysterious then!

If the 'ya' is not the shortened form of either 'yeah' or 'you', then what is it? Honestly, even I don't know. However, what I do know is that it is not grammatically apt to end sentences with 'ya'. You will never find native speakers of English say that.

I have a feeling we say it owing to our habit of saying something similar in our mother tongues. Here is an example:

छोड़ न यार *(chowd na yaar;* literally, Hindi for 'forget it, friend')

If you prod someone to sing, you can easily expect a response like:

मत कर ना यार! मुझे गाना बिल्कुल नहीं आता *(mut kur naa yaar! Muzhay gaanaa bilkool nahi aata;* literally, Hindi for 'Please don't, buddy! I cannot sing at all.')

In a more formal context, native speakers would simply use words like 'son', 'dear', 'my friend', etc. Colloquially, they are known to use words like 'bro', 'dude', 'mate' or the dozens of other options, depending on the region and the dialect.

Culprit and solution found then. Case closed!

## 108

## *Yeh Dil Mange More*

*Yeh dil mange more!* Today, everybody wants more out of everything, and perhaps justifiably so. After all, aren't we all living in the day and age of the consumer? But there are times when having more won't always be possible until someone really important does not change the rules of the game (read grammar).

We are talking about how some people use 'more' incorrectly in the comparative degree, a degree used to compare two persons or two things; for example:

*'This garden is bigger than that one.'*

Or,

*'Tom is taller than Tim.'*

The comparative degree is usually formed by adding the suffix '-er' to an adjective (big becomes big<u>er</u>, tall becomes tall<u>er</u>). However, certain adjectives do not take the suffix '-er'; for example, 'beautiful'. One tends to use 'more' before such adjectives in the comparative degree; for example:

*'This flower is more beautiful than that one.'*

Then, there are some adjectives that change completely in the comparative and superlative degrees, for example 'good' (positive degree), 'better' (comparative degree) and 'best' (superlative degree). And this is where the problem with the use of the word 'more' seems to occur the most.

It is not uncommon to hear people say, 'more pretty' (when saying 'prettier' is an option) or even say 'more better' (when they should actually be using only 'better').

These mistakes are perhaps a reflection of the influence of our mother tongues. Here are some examples:

ज्यादा अच्छा (*jyaadaa achchaa;* literally, Hindi for 'more better')

बहुत ज्यादा खूबसूरत *(bahoot jyaadaa khoobsoorat;* literally, Hindi for 'very more pretty')

વધારે સારું *(vadhaaray saroo;* literally, Gujarati for 'more better')

વધારે સુંદર *(vadhaaray soondar;* literally, Gujarati for 'more pretty')

And by the way, 'more' is a versatile word that can be used as a determiner, as in:

*'I poured myself more tea.'*

As a pronoun, as in:

*'He knows more than me.'*

And as an adverb, as in:

*'I like mutton more than chicken.'*

Let me leave you with this! The more you know about 'more', the more helpful it would be to know when to use 'more' or less of 'more'.

## 109

# Toilet Woes

The mention of toilets often makes me think of the dozen quirks people have when it comes to doing their daily business. Some will simply not feel the pressure unless they have a cup of tea, while some others need a cigarette before things get going. Then, there are those who cannot perform the act if there is too much silence, and some others who need a newspaper while things take their natural course.

There is no dearth of quirks as there is no dearth of names that we have attributed to this sacred place that we visit every morning. Most of us call it a 'toilet', but then you will also hear people call it by other names, like the cool-sounding 'loo', the primitive-sounding 'WC' (short for 'water closet'), the conventional-sounding 'bathroom' and 'lavatory', or the clear favourites in every starred hotel and restaurant—the 'restroom' and the 'washroom'.

Looks like options galore, but that is not quite true because these words have distinct meanings and thereby distinct usage. The word 'loo', for example, means the same as 'toilet' but can only be used informally. And although people might imagine the entire room when they hear these two words, both 'loo' and 'toilet' technically only mean the 'pot' (known as a 'commode' in Indian English).

Technicalities apart, one can use the words 'toilet' and 'loo' in common parlance when referring to a pot or a space containing one. And that is how it works with the word 'WC' too, although its usage is less common as compared to the former two. A WC is a type of toilet, but one that has an inbuilt flush. It means the pot but can also be used to refer to the room that houses one. Speaking of rooms, there are 'washrooms' and 'restrooms' too.

In American English, a 'washroom' is a room that has a toilet as well as facilities for washing, whereas a 'restroom' is a toilet that is in a public building. To the British, however, a washroom would mean nothing, while a restroom would still be a room in a public building but one that is meant for people to relax, not one that has toilets.

As for a 'bathroom', it is the most comprehensive type of room—one that contains a shower, a washbasin and a toilet. Americans and Brits seem to agree on the meaning of this one, although they differ again when it comes to a 'lavatory'. To the Americans, a lavatory is a washbasin in a bathroom, but to the Brits it is simply a synonym of WC.

Phew! Who would have thought there was so much grammar to our biology?

## 110

# Yes and No

You could seem like a totally different person to someone who does not speak your language. That is probably why Philippe, our French guest, found my Indian friend to be very shy. In reality, he is a pedigreed brat who can get on your nerves and under your skin, all at once. The only reason he appeared shy was because he spoke neither French nor English.

But that is scary, right? It means people might form incorrect opinions about us, depending on how and what we say, and whether we say anything at all. Indians are generally known to be docile, obedient and well-mannered people. However, those perceptions could change the moment we speak a different language.

Sample this! The average Indian, when asked if they want something, let us say some tea, would respond with a plain and simple 'yes' or 'no' in English. At best, we might consider adding something like a 'sure', a 'why not', or an 'absolutely' to our affirmative answer, or a 'just had some' to our negative answer.

Turns out, responding with just a 'yes' or a 'no' will come across as rude to the natives. Oh damn! That is terrible because we do not mean to be rude. How do we make the right impression, then? Well, just do what they do. Simple! Natives always respond with a 'yes, please' or a 'no, thank you'.

So, the next time you need to answer a yes–no question, you know what not to forget. So much for coming across as the courteous people we truly are.

### '(Your name) This Side'

Like there are two sides to a coin, there are two sides to even a phone call it seems. That is perhaps why some people introduce themselves as, 'Hello Sir! Mallika this side.' Why complicate things? Just simply say, 'this is Mallika' or 'my name is Mallika'.

## Acknowledgements

Writing this book has been like having a baby without needing to go through the labour. Authors spend months researching for a book. In comparison, my life was made easy by the millions of Indians who use English in their day-to-day lives. All I had to do was keep my ears and eyes wide open. It took 15 long years of compulsive observing, but the content just kept coming to me. A heartfelt thank you to every English-speaking Indian who has unknowingly contributed in the making of this book.

At times, the English we speak is influenced by how things are said in our mother tongues. In chapters that talk about such Indianisms, I have cited examples in Bengali, Gujarati, Hindi, Kannada, Konkani, Marathi and Punjabi, since I claim varied degrees of skills in each one of them. A sincere thank you to Dona Sihi, Kaushik Joshi, Ankita Kesari, Srinidhi T.G., Kshama Dharwadkar and Harjinder Singh for helping me validate the accuracy of the examples in your respective languages, and that too at odd hours.

This book is as much an effort to laugh at our own expense as it is to take the opportunity to share with all of you how the natives say it. In that sense, I could not have written this book without having a native English speaker to lean on. Thank you, Claudia Bragman, for patiently answering my naively native questions, for allowing me to nudge and push you for answers, and for never being brief in your explanations.

No matter how many times you read the manuscript, you still need a pair of eyes you can trust, eyes that will not only spot the tiniest of errors but also act as your candid critics, helping you make sense of what is good and what is not, especially when too much writing has killed all objectivity. My wife, Nandita, and my very dear friends, Alifya Thingna and Anoop Deshpande—all accomplished and hugely experienced language professionals themselves—I cannot thank you enough for your invaluable inputs, constructive criticisms and reassuring words.

Being a book for all ages, I needed to know how it would be received by an age group that I had stopped belonging to long ago, the teenagers. My daughter, Sía Nulkar, herself a voracious reader, played that role to perfection, contributing not only with insights but also with content and corrections. Thank you, Sía!

Then, a very special mention of the ones but for whom this book would have stayed a mere manuscript. Thank you, Rudra Sharma and Rupa Publications, for believing in this book. Rudra, thank you for all the conversations that might have seemed like just another day at work for you but meant the world to me. Your words gave me the clarity and direction that made this book possible.

Most importantly, thank you Sagareeka Pradhan. Your eye for detail and insightful suggestions have added great value to the book and made it look so perfect in every sense.

And finally, thank you to the divine force that continues to manifest itself in more ways than one, just so that we never stop believing that magic does indeed happen.

Divinely blessed, eternally grateful!

# Glossary of Grammatical Terms

**Abbreviation**: A shortened form of a word or a phrase

**Adjective Phrase**: A group of words that gives more information about a noun or pronoun

**Adjective**: A word that gives more information about the noun

**Adverb**: A word that gives more information about the verb

**Collocation**: A pair of words used together

**Conjugation**: The variation of the spelling of the verb depending on the subject

**Definite Article**: A word that introduces previously mentioned, commonly known or specific nouns

**Direct Object**: A noun phrase denoting a person or thing that is the recipient of the action of a transitive verb

**Exclamation**: A sudden cry or remark expressing surprise, strong emotion or pain

**Genericised Trademark**: A trademark that has become the generic name for a general class of products or services

**Imperative Tag**: Questions, statements or imperatives that are added to a clause to encourage a response from the listener

**Intensive Pronoun**: A word that lays stress on the pronoun it refers back to

**Intransitive Verb**: A verb that does not need a direct object (for example, a noun or a pronoun) to complete its meaning

**Logogram**: A sign or character representing a word or a phrase

**Noun**: A word that identifies people, places or things

**Phrase**: A group of words standing together as a conceptual unit

**Pleonasm**: The use of more words than are necessary to convey the meaning

**Preposition**: A word that tells you where or when something is in relation to something else

**Present Participle**: The form of the verb ending in '-ing'

**Pronoun**: A word that replaces a noun or noun phrase

**Regular Verb**: A verb that follows the normal pattern of conjugation

**Statement Tag**: An informal, affirmative tag that's added to the end of a declarative sentence

**Suffix**: Letters added at the end of a word to form a derivative

**Synonym**: Words with the same meaning

**Transitive Verb**: A verb that needs a direct object (for example, a noun or a pronoun) to complete its meaning

**Universal Tag**: Informal words that are used to add emphasis or reinforcement to an affirmative statement

**Verb**: A word that describes an action, a state or an occurrence

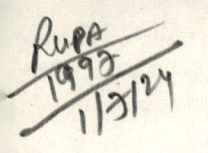